Reverend Father Doctorandus M
(15.11.1997 - 15.11.2022), Volume 1. ...

Reverend Father Doctorandus Maurice Akwa: 25th Priestly Anniversary Festschrift (15.11.1997 - 15.11.2022): From Weh-Wum to Bertoua and the United States of America, Life, Works, Tributes, Good Will Messages, and Immortal Literary Legacies, Volume 1
With a Goodwill Message from Bishop Michael Francis Burbidge, Bishop of the Diocese of Arlington, Virginia, USA

Altruistic Pastor of Souls; Scholarly and Avid Pastoral Clinical Psychotherapist; Inexhaustible Biblical Scholar and Magister; Famed Former Secretary for Catholic Education; Preeminent Major Seminary Lecturer and Spiritual Director; Erudite Spiritual Year Rector; Memorable Diocesan Spiritual Director for Catholic Men and Women's Associations; Celebrated Diocesan Ecumenical Coordinator; Prominent Chaplain and Coordinator of the Association of Widows and Orphans; Outstanding Basketball Coach; Distinguished Student University President; Well-known Dramatist; Legendary Priest with a Passion for the Sick, Underprivileged and the Aging; Cherished Former Sacred Heart College Mankon Teacher; The Peoples Father (Pater Populi); Choir Conductor par Excellence; and Prolific Writer of Biblical Reflections.
Edited by Nchumbonga George Lekelefac

Reverend Father Doctorandus Maurice Akwa: 25th Priestly Anniversary Festschrift (15.11.1997 - 15.11.2022), Volume 1. Edited by Nchumbonga George Lekelefac

Copyright © Nchumbonga George Lekelefac, 2022
Contact Information:
Nchumbonga George Lekelefac
Nchumbonga Lekelefac Institute of Research, Documentation, Language and Culture, USA
Oklahoma City, Oklahoma State, USA
Email: nchumbong@yahoo.com

Tel: 203. 726. 5241

First published: 2022

All rights reserved

No part of this publication may be reproduced, photocopied, photographed or transmitted in any form or by any means, without the express written permission from the author.

Researched and Published by the "Nchumbonga Lekelefac Institute of Research, Documentation, Language and Culture, USA". Oklahoma City, Oklahoma State, USA

Reverend Father Doctorandus Maurice Akwa: 25th Priestly Anniversary Festschrift (15.11.1997 - 15.11.2022), Volume 1. Edited by Nchumbonga George Lekelefac

Table of Content

Dedication 60

Good will Message from Bishop Michael Francis Burbidge, bishop of the Diocese of Arlington, in Virginia, USA 60

Introduction 70

Chapter One: Biography of Reverend Father Maurice Akwa ... 78

Chapter Two: 25th Anniversary Wishes from Well Wishers and Friends 81

1. Agbor Michael Ashu 81
2. Gladys Obale 81
3. Priscilla Neng Mulesiwi 81
4. Mbunwe Colette 81
5. Natang Yong 81
6. Paulette Synajie 82
7. Lydia Ekeme 82
8. Jasper Nuh 82
9. Auntiefaus Nimongum 82

10. Alice Suika 82
11. Viviana Aguii 82
12. Lemnyuy Dora 82
13. Joh Cecilia 83
14. Therese Mezigue 83
15. Martin Jumbam 83
16. Kang Lucia 83
17. Hedrine Tamajong 83
18. Sheila Forbi 83
19. Edna Fonban 83
20. Mvomo Michel 84
21. Nathalie Lydienne Mekongo 84
22. Ntumnafoinkom Patience Sama Ndi 84
23. Nkwain Juliana 84
24. Yega Elizabeth 84
25. Jinoh Jamet Banjong 84
26. Banye Sivla Mary 85
27. Mvo Prudencia 85
28. Ngekwi Betty 85
29. Nju Christopher 85
30. Millbrigg Simon Spencer 85
31. Brandino Kuwong 85
32. Colette Mbengon Meboma 85
33. Marceline Yele 86
34. Florence Uche 86

35. Ngwa Mary Anne 86
36. Banboye Blandine Bongmoyong 86
37. Maceline MB 86
38. Abah Quinta 87
39. Ntonoh Belinda 87
40. Nju Christopher 87
41. Debora Ngonbossom Kiringa 87
42. Mbanga Rose 87
43. Bernardine Audrey Yaya Wirnkar 87
44. Taminang Pierre 87
45. Elizabeth Mbayu 88
46. Nsoseka Loveline Leinyuy 88
47. Oben Afah 88
48. Yvy Bebe Darl 88
49. Biddy Kaspa 88
50. Jeannette Moubitang 88
51. Agnes Mbongere 89
52. Brigitte Ngoyang 89
53. Lydia Nanga 89
54. Judith Ngum 89
55. Mimi La Belle 89
56. Ngulefac Fondong 89
57. George Nchumbonga Lekelefac 89
58. Elizabeth Wachong 90
59. Ebonlo Grace 90

60. George Nchumbonga Lekelefac 90
61. Belinda Chungong 90
62. Agem Clement Ebua 90
63. Wendy Ngong 90
64. Mambo Ngu 90
65. Edith Ngwa 91
66. Erika Indira Zara 91
67. Jessie Nchuo 91
68. Rose Vershiyi 91
69. Ngwefuni Max Igna 91
70. Wirsiy Yujika 91
71. Judith Forfir 91
72. Victor Nformi 92
73. Cornelia Echike Kwekam 92
74. Immaculate Che 92
75. Ernestine Besong 92
76. Grace Fombe 92
77. Simon Nguepi 92
78. Cloudatte Akwen 92
79. Doris Bei 93
80. Florence Asaah Keng 93
81. Mawo Regine 93
82. Pammella Ngefor 93
83. Odette Mbie 93
84. Maurice Akwa 93

85. Gnintedem Hugette Temgoua 93
86. Duchess K Lira 94
87. Julet Okafor 94
88. Jeogras Ntube 94
89. Raymond Assila 94
90. Loreta Yah 94
91. Njua Christina 94
92. Assumpta Aba 94
93. Lidwina Kroll 95
94. Gilda Ryan Ewang Ngwesse 95
95. Gus Bessong 95
96. Pamela Tegha 95
97. Caroline Tcheffo 95
98. Mary Mah 95
99. Racheal Atanga 96
100. Mary Njah Foncham 96
101. Nicolyne Fonjie Idem 96
102. Angelica Bih 96
103. Roseline Nasih 96
104. Beatrice Moma 96
105. Bakia Anjie 97
106. Paul Ken Asobo 97
107. Bernice Yong 97
108. Ncham Emma 97
109. MultiTasker Numéro-Uno 97

Reverend Father Doctorandus Maurice Akwa: 25th Priestly Anniversary Festschrift (15.11.1997 - 15.11.2022), Volume 1. Edited by Nchumbonga George Lekelefac

110. Maurice Akwa 97
111. Martha Ketchu 98
112. Cho Che Ivo 98
113. La Grace de Dieu 98
114. Ibeanuka Ife Callista Chukwuma 98
115. Gwanmesia Pamela Bakoh 98
116. Henry Mua 98
117. Nkamsi Besong 99
118. Hilda Ndumu 99
119. Therese Binfon 99
120. Kejetue Perpetua 99
121. Jane Mobufor 99
122. Catherine Atesiri Ambe 99
123. Electa Nsabin 100
124. Florence Kouchou 100
125. Prosper Wang Tih Besibang 100
126. Kongnso Prudencia 100
127. Ndum Juliana 100
128. Kintang Dufe 100
129. Maggie Egbe 100
130. Marie Effa 101
131. Gwendoline Atabong Nkumbah 101
132. Father Maurice Akwa 101
133. Caroline Asongwe Cho-Nji 101
134. Timkain Shella 102

135. Love Teumo 102
136. Juliette Nde 102
137. Viviana Auguri 102
138. Ethel Chu Buh 102
139. Gigi Akwa 102
140. Ngwinui Juliana 103
141. Fai Wookitaav 103
142. Vera Liku 103
143. Bin Alice 103
144. Marcelline Foncham 103
145. Ewane Mary 103
146. Marcelline Foncham 103
147. Lydia Ekeme 104
148. Sabina Jules 104
149. Nina Mezu-Nwaba 104
150. Fumbii Caroline Ankiambom Niba 104
151. Miranda Ikfi 104
152. Zou Evelyn 104
153. Divine Nchamukong 104
154. Cloudatte Akwen 105
155. Bame Evelyn 105
156. Nein Eveline 105
157. Yaah Maggie Kilo 105
158. Mvo Prudencia 105
159. Ntumnafoinkom Patience Sama Ndi 105

160. Shura F. Ursula 106
161. Julius Ngole 106
162. Rose Vershiyi 106
163. Julet Okafor 106
164. Ngwa Martin 106
165. Kongnso Prudencia 106
166. Jean-françois Ebah 107
167. Mbanga Rose 107
168. Cornelia Echike Kwekam 107
169. Christie Ngale 107
170. Ebony Shudelphine 107
171. Elian Mambo 107
172. Olachi Joy Mezu-Ndubuisi 108
173. Victor Nformi 108
174. Fonguh Bih 108
175. Lawrence Eyabi 108
176. Kilian Waindim 108
177. Yaya Yvette 108
178. Mvomo Michel 109
179. Elizabeth Wachong 109
180. Nicolyne Fonjie Idem 109
181. Fille Pygmée Badia 109
182. Michael Mua 109
183. Anjifua Ntonghanwah 109
184. Nkwain Juliana 109

185. Flore Kabiyene 110
186. Constance Kemeyong Megouya 110
187. Elodie A. Tendoh 110
188. Marlyse Mbanga 110
189. Nju Ghong Mercy Mbong 110
190. Tegha Ajemawen Amaazee 110
191. Agbor Michael Ashu 111
192. Anthony Ateh 111
193. Millbrigg Simon Spencer 111
194. Prodencia Asaba 111
195. Anne Francis 111
196. Maceline MB 111
197. Mbah Rene 112
198. Eveline Babah Mbuh 112
199. Beri Nyuy 112
200. Lawong Yula 112
201. Jane Mobufor 112
202. Nnang Mathias 112
203. Priscilla Neng Mulesiwi 113
204. Patrick Fohneng Seh 113
205. Hakeem Noibi 113
206. Edna Fonban 113
207. Patricia Fornishi 113
208. Daniel Ache 113
209. Jevis Mai-Akwa 113

210. Mua Anna Itung 114
211. Maggi Akwa 114
212. Abang Emmanuel Toh 114
213. F Junior Kings 114
214. Vivianne Hortense Matchouanbou 114
215. Cinta Chia 114
216. Kang Lucia 114
217. Anne Waindim 115
218. Ngufor Delphine 115
219. Nji Jude 115
220. Emilienne Lavine Lobe 115
221. Therese Songwoua 115
222. Eta Oben 115
223. Elvire Obame 115
224. Careen Nyang 116
225. Henriette Mengue 116
226. Gabby M. C. Joseph-Ibe 116
227. Regina Tante 116
228. Seh Gladys 116
229. Celestine Tume 116
230. Mbunwe Colette 116
231. Jeannette Moubitang 117
232. Whitney Braids Besinga 117
233. Grace Asaba 117
234. Mungang Endless 117

235. Etty Tams 117
236. Patience Enow 117
237. Eddy Etawo 118
238. Bernardine Audrey Yaya Wirnkar 118
239. Banboye Blandine Bongmoyong 118
240. Duchess K Lira 118
241. Larrisa Azeteh 118
242. Grace Fombe 118
243. Nann Emigold 119
244. Mbeng Anthony 119
245. Dymphna Maybelle S 119
246. Tonain Tonain 119
247. Natang Yong 119
248. James Asonglefac 119
249. Electra Ngum 119
250. Étoile Du Matin 120
251. Karin Awa 120
252. Peter Suh-Nfor Tangyie 120
253. Magdalene Orock 120
254. Colette Mbengon Meboma 120
255. Colette Mbengon Meboma 121
256. Kebei Susan 121
257. Michael Boyo 121
258. Immaculate Chongwain Tedji 121
259. Brenda Tang 121

260. Wirsiy Yujika 121
261. Mbandi Caro 121
262. Loreta Yah 122
263. Nicoline Chomilo 122
264. Ngu Azeh 122
265. Bong Akwa 122
266. Lidwina Kroll 122
267. Rosemary Love 122
268. Nini Bih 122
269. B-k Marie-Paris 123
270. Jane Bebs 123
271. Joy Kahmou 123
272. Sih Enyowe 123
273. Mike Munro 123
274. Darlin Joan 123
275. Ngwa Angeline 124
276. Solange Minka 124
277. Janet Pfeffer 124
278. Buma Wilfred 124
279. Fonkenmun Samjella Edwin 124
280. Caroline Tenye 124
281. Collette Ngante 124
282. Neba Veritas Ngum 125
283. Emmanuel Moma Kisob 125
284. Tata Viola 125

285. Mac Fornishi 125
286. Angelica Bih 125
287. Pepe Kuchah 125
288. Rose Mezu 125
289. Asaba Lylian 126
290. Kinyuy Nyuysemo 126
291. Pam Pam 126
292. Chebe Wai 126
293. Ntaintain Nyiaseh 126
294. Sheila Forbi 126
295. Nkongho Lucy Enoru 126
296. Ewee Pamela Zuo 127
297. Nash Nathalia 127
298. Shey Limmy Dubila 127
299. Agnes Mbongere 127
300. Ando Casi 127
301. Wallang Ernest 127
302. Anang Grace 127
303. Abah Quinta 128
304. Belle Sonkey 128
305. Lem Ndiangang 128
306. Ngum Evy 128
307. Hedrine Tamajong 128
308. Biks Biks 128
309. Mbong Mih 129

310. Suika Ishatou 129
311. Emilia Nde Ambe-Niba 129
312. Rita Biedenharn 129
313. Daniel Tsague 129
314. Auntiefaus Nimongum 129
315. Netty Ekukole 129
316. Juliette Menga 130
317. Marian Mua 130
318. Mildrate Nnam 130
319. Elizabeth Mbayu 130
320. Njua Christina 130
321. Maa Ade Abumbi II 130
322. Berthe Amboo 130
323. Francis Ebeke 131
324. Biddy Kaspa 131
325. Bertila Kongnyuy 131
326. Mary Asoh 131
327. Francis Ebeke 131
328. Yvonne Fondufe-Mittendorf 131
329. Charlotte Akenji 131
330. Anna Ngu 132
331. Median Fomonyuy Wirkom 132
332. Evelyn Bridget 132
333. Besongha Zembeh 132
334. Oben Afah 132

335. Mabel Nkembeng 133
336. Karen Giermek 133
337. Magalie Pierre Keil 133
338. Alexander Binnyuy Ngalim 133
339. Hycentha Lai 133
340. Brunhilda Asamba 133
341. Assumpta Aba 133
342. Gene Tetuh 134
343. Esubat Fonkeng 134
344. Jemimah Chuks 134
345. Ojong Roseline Nkongho 134
346. Frida Ngu 134
347. Augustine Bikim 134
348. Augustine Bikim 135
349. Rosy Touh 135
350. Ngoum Jovita 135
351. Bertha Waindim 135
352. Kel MNnbu 135
353. Jemia Asobo A Minang 135
354. Gus Bessong 135
355. Winifred Leogaa Fofuleng 136
356. Rita N Fang 136
357. Nkukuma Edjoa 136
358. Rita Cham 136
359. Yvonne Standley 136

360. Cho Nji Stephen 136
361. Ebonlo Grace 137
362. Jinoh Jamet Banjong 137
363. Sofa Bertila 137
364. Janice Hoover-Durel 137
365. Chris Fokumlah 137
366. Pauline Asobo 137
367. Chimène Nlong 137
368. Kum Edith Ewo 138
369. Nicholine Ndikum 138
370. Brian H. Reynolds 138
371. Bertrand Tchoumi 138
372. Viban Helen 138
373. MC Christabell Tanteh 138
374. Anthonia Chenyi 139
375. Roseta Ade 139
376. Geraldine Tar 139
377. Ngulefac Fondong 139
378. Mandy Fonkeng 139
379. Mary Takwa 139
380. Wisdom Elizabeth 139
381. Kuna Flo 140
382. Mah Fidelia 140
383. Ernestine Besong 140
384. Bei Adela Kpu 140

385. Pride Funju 140
386. Mike-Anne Waters 140
387. Jacqueline Nju-Ghong 140
388. Michael Gorman 141
389. Rachel Ojong 141
390. Margaret Sihmeg 141
391. Adel Etia 141
392. Giesel Kemani 141
393. Mbanga Paul Ngwa 141
394. Vita Donvialli 141
395. Priscilla Woye 142
396. Margaret Fogam 142
397. Apollonia Bongwir 142
398. Rose Achoh 142
399. Patience Mbonifor 142
400. Ntonoh Belinda 142
401. Mimi Ambe 143
402. Sina Gbake 143
403. Erika Indira Zara 143
404. Gladys Lantum Achiri 143
405. Grace Ngum Awantu 143
406. Mispa Lachris 143
407. Mimi La Belle 144
408. Cinta Chia 144
409. Mathias Akih 144

Reverend Father Doctorandus Maurice Akwa: 25th Priestly Anniversary Festschrift (15.11.1997 - 15.11.2022), Volume 1. Edited by Nchumbonga George Lekelefac

410. Nkenyi Claris 144
411. Yega Elizabeth 144
412. Swiri Rose Saningong 144
413. Helen Tambe 144
414. Martha F. Langdon 145
415. Niba-Ahlijah Meh Niba-Ahlijah 145
416. Betty Schmedes 145
417. Yvonne Nyambi 145
418. Hen Ndatchi Mayikith 145
419. Ernestine Esambe 145
420. Laura Ngwana 145
421. Wan Lii 146
422. Lucille Munchi 146
423. Immaculate Che 146
424. Kinyuy Forgwe 146
425. Kinyuy Forgwe 146
426. Martina Atabong 146
427. Ban John Beghabe Blaise 146
428. Stella Fonbod 147
429. Ginny Rauer 147
430. Mbonifor Emilia 147
431. Nsoseka Loveline Leinyuy 147
432. Dominic Forka 147
433. Justine Ma 147
434. Rosemary Niba 147

435. Mirabel Ngum 148
436. Nkah Leonard 148
437. Mabel Ndum 148
438. Marcel Enah 148
439. Karen Ali Tayong 148
440. Gnintedem Hugette Temgoua 148
441. Quinta Sangha 148
442. Michael C. Yuh 149
443. Mary Florence Chia 149
444. Bessem Ojong 149
445. Joahana Mambo Tingem-Locker 149
446. Atumbhai Nain 149
447. Rosimex Ndasi 149
448. Zeel Patel 150
449. Geraldine Tumenta 150
450. Geraldine Tumenta 150
451. Geraldine Tumenta 150
452. Emelda Lipawah Ngwanyia-Anangfack 150
453. Gladys Elad 150
454. Gladys Elad 150
455. Pamela Tegha 151
456. Eunice Gwanmesia 151
457. Caroline Mpako 151
458. Pascal Tantoh 151
459. Julia Buban Ngu 151

460. Wiysola Gilly 151
461. Naomi Blessings 152
462. Noela Gift 152
463. Lawrence Yong 152
464. Ngulefac Prodencia 152
465. Sarah Maier 152
466. Stella Wanki 152
467. Gwanmesia Pamela Bakoh 153
468. Mary Chilla 153
469. Clemantine Fonkeng 153
470. Simon Buh 153
471. Leonie Mpafe Samuto 153
472. Mathias Njong 153
473. Pamela Bah 154
474. Pamela Bah 154
475. Cham Odette 154
476. Jacqueline Mukala Wainfein 154
477. Oliver Asaah 154
478. Tabi Irine 154
479. Dominican Monastery Bambui 154
480. Emelda Ngwe 155
481. Erika Wright 155
482. Mbong Marie Kembo 155
483. Chanty Moore 155
484. Taminang Pierre 155

485. Ndidi Anozie Sr. 155
486. Marie Wankah 155
487. Gisele Mofor 156
488. Nji Rosaline 156
489. Adèle Essama 156
490. Beatrice Moma 156
491. Anselm Kebei 156
492. Mbei Bridget 156
493. Ndifor Winifred 157
494. Victorine Ambe Dwamina 157
495. Euphemia Mah 157
496. Edward Cheng 157
497. Stephen Tanjang 157
498. Nenge Azefor Njongmeta 157
499. Angie Owih 157
500. Cecilia Awasum 158
501. Asonglefac Nkemleke 158
502. Felicitas Ayuk 158
503. George Nchumbonga-Chrysostom Lekelefac 158
504. Ewoh Nathalie 158
505. Odilia Fri Mundi Wankwi 158
506. Kate Ngeloh 159
507. Nkeng Ajua Alemanji 159
508. Gabriel Asaba 159
509. Dione Amarantha 159

Reverend Father Doctorandus Maurice Akwa: 25th Priestly Anniversary Festschrift (15.11.1997 - 15.11.2022), Volume 1. Edited by Nchumbonga George Lekelefac

510. Dominica Ngante 159
511. Maurice Akwa 159
512. Pam Miye 160
513. Doc Mafor 160
514. Lilian Ngwana Banmi 160
515. Huguette Flore Okole 160
516. Godfred Kah Mbali 160
517. Tim Finnian 160
518. Mambo Ngu 160
519. Belinda Chungong 161
520. Laure Amougou 161
521. Chi Alice 161
522. Ngwa Jude 161
523. Ngwa Jude 161
524. Yvonne Boma 161
525. Felicia Nyambi 161
526. Sam Brunhilda 162
527. Gladys Ntang Vusi 162
528. Clara Chimasa Kien 162
529. Lambert Mbom 162
530. Maurice Akwa 162
531. Ngono Marguerite 162
532. Gladys Obale 163
533. Cynthia Norris 163
534. Ernest Yemene 163

535. Monice Roca Ntatin 163
536. Pierre Magouga Mahele 163
537. Eveline Mbonifor-Mba 163
538. Maurice Akwa 163
539. Rose Rose 164
540. Mispa Nkematabong 164
541. Wendy Ngong 164
542. Fuh Doreen Manka 164
543. Stella Juo Kum 164
544. Eve Fornishi 164
545. Julius Tuma 165
546. Pruddy Ghong 165
547. Priscilla Wankie 165
548. Nicole Iknicky 165
549. Paulette Synajie 165
550. Hycenta Njua 165
551. Joh Cecilia 165
552. Missmill Akene 166
553. Ndum Juliana 166
554. Suhtah Bangang 166
555. Christine Ngangsic 166
556. Bridget Beng 166
557. Evelyn Bah 166
558. Massalla Irene 166
559. Ngono Son 167

560. Gakehmi Florence 167
561. Florence Forghab Formum 167
562. Chiatoh Collins Songbi 167
563. Richard Fobella 167
564. Tonjock Cecil 167
565. Clarence Ndangam 168
566. Zida Mua 168
567. Doris Bei 168
568. Bridgette Kangsen 168
569. Juskall Meedocktorr 168
570. Kintang Dufe 168
571. Lady-Cel Cornelia EladLambe 169
572. Jessie Nchuo 169
573. Cyril Ngwa 169
574. Angelica Bih 169
575. Chinje Loveline 169
576. Gertrude Tabuwe Sirri Ngongba 169
577. Angelica Bih 169
578. Jack Ballad 170
579. Electa Nsabin 170
580. Lucille Munchi 170
581. Eveline Ncho 170
582. Suika Ishatou 170
583. Ewarre Vanessa 170
584. Régine Atangana 170

585. Loreta Yah 171
586. Chi Gillian 171
587. Ambe Sergius 171
588. Mbanga Rose 171
589. Gertrude Tabuwe Sirri Ngongba 171
590. Paulette Synajie 171
591. Atumbhai Nain 171
592. Ebony Shudelphine 172
593. Ndeh Lum Eucharia 172
594. Bernardine Audrey Yaya Wirnkar 172
595. Angelica Bih 172
596. Magdalene Orock 172
597. Rel Rel 172
598. Maggi Akwa 172
599. Shura F. Ursula 173
600. Che Gillian Mbei 173
601. Anselm Kebei 173
602. Bernardine Audrey Yaya Wirnkar 173
603. Pruddy Ghong 173
604. Olachi Joy Mezu-Ndubuisi 173
605. Priscilla Neng Mulesiwi 173
606. Eveline Ncho 174
607. Tah Claire Bright 174
608. Asenath Asang 174
609. Gabriel Asaba 174

610. Elizabeth Mbayu 174
611. Roseta Ade 174
612. Njua Christina 174
613. Marlyse Mbanga 175
614. Roseline Nasih 175
615. Rita N Fang 175
616. Mbanga Rose 175
617. Rosy Touh 175
618. Yvonne Fondufe-Mittendorf 175
619. Ibeanuka Ife Callista Chukwuma 175
620. Jean Pierre Lteif 176
621. Eugenie Nkemka 176
622. Mike-Anne Waters 176
623. Ngulefac Fondong 176
624. Maurine Lukong 176
625. Angelica Bih 176
626. Laura Ngwana 177
627. RoseMary Ngehsab Lum 177
628. Eunice Gwanmesia 177
629. Sheila Forbi 177
630. Rosy Touh 177
631. Mary Florence Chia 177
632. Ewane Mary 177
633. Karen Ali Tayong 178
634. Dr-Marcelline Nyambi 178

635. Emmanuel Moma Kisob 178
636. Aggie Elangwe 178
637. Clotilde Ngante 178
638. Wisdom Elizabeth 178
639. E Nah Gwanmesia 179
640. Kela Delphine Njike-Tah 179
641. Emma Yenla Elame 179
642. Immaculate Che 179
643. Gus Bessong 179
644. Duchess K Lira 179
645. Victorine Ambe Dwamina 180
646. Janice Hoover-Durel 180
647. Ethel Bih 180
648. Manso Arrey 180
649. Lucie Ngongbo 180
650. Beatrice Tangeh 180
651. Bih Marian 180
652. Tanwani Esther 181
653. Angelbert Chikere 181
654. Assumpta Aba 181
655. Timothy Clasen 181
666. Abang Emmanuel Toh 181
667. Biddy Kaspa 182
668. Mbei Bridget 182
669. Godfred Kah Mbali 182

670. Maryline Shang Nformi 182
671. Florence Forghab Formum 182
672. Nicoline Chomilo 182
673. Ojong Roseline Nkongho 182
674. Paulette Synajie 183
675. Fonguh Bih 183
676. Mua Anna Itung 183
677. Caroline Tenye 183
678. Fumbii Caroline Ankiambom Niba 183
679. Gnintedem Hugette Temgoua 183
680. Christie Ngale 184
681. Mbatsogo Kamte Maureen 184
682. Gertrude Tabuwe Sirri Ngongba 184
683. Lizette Tumasang 184
684. Chiatoh Collins Songbi 184
685. Grace Ngum Awantu 184
686. Bertila Kongnyuy 184
687. Florence Tumasang 185
688. Mathias Njong 185
689. Median Fomonyuy Wirkom 185
690. Yvonne Tum 185
691. Evelyn Bah 185
692. Auntiefaus Nimongum 185
693. Juliana S Asuku 185
694. Irene Pechase 186

695. Judith Bi Suh 186
696. Jocelyn Zinkeng 186
697. Josephine Niba Awounfac 186
698. Josephine Niba Awounfac 186
699. Gladys Ntang Vusi 186
700. Bernadette Atanga 186
701. Gemma Abonge 187
702. Vivian Acha-Morfaw 187
703. Cloudatte Akwen 187
704. Bernardine Audrey Yaya Wirnkar 187
705. Asanji Niba 187
706. Kah Rogers 187
707. Régine Atangana 187
708. Maceline MB 188
709. Taniform Taniform 188
710. Ngwa Mary Anne 188
711. Zie Nji Atang 188
712. Kelly Prudence 188
713. Naomi Blessings 188
714. Hedrine Tamajong 188
715. Chia Frederick Yong 189
716. Bibiana Tita 189
717. Shey Don Dubila 189
718. Selamo Rene Suinyuy 189
719. Nini Bih 189

720. Ntaintain Nyiaseh ... 189
721. Delphine Nsen Njukwe ... 189
722. Rita Cham ... 190
723. Beatrice Tangeh ... 190
724. Beatrice Moma ... 190
725. Assumpta Aba ... 190
726. Paulette Synajie ... 190
727. Elias Bisong ... 190
728. Agnes Mbongere ... 190
729. Gnintedem Hugette Temgoua ... 191
730. Angelica Bih ... 191
731. Gertrude Tabuwe Sirri Ngongba ... 191
732. Evelyn Bah ... 191
733. Josephine Niba Awounfac ... 191
734. Maurice Akwa ... 191
735. Prince Garba Splendor ... 191
736. Abram Mario ... 192
737. Pierrot Amougou Zambo ... 192
738. Vernyuy Nsaikila Gabriel Alexis ... 192
739. Etiendem Valentine ... 192
740. Killeng Styve ... 192
741. Ndemtchu Solange ... 192
742. Rita Biedenharn ... 192
743. Priscilla Neng Mulesiwi ... 193
744. Immaculate Che ... 193

745. Neba Celestine Asombang 193
746. Steve Angafor 193
747. Yvonne Boma 193
748. Irene Kijem 193
749. Immaculate Che 193
750. Abine Florence Bih 194
751. Divine Nchamukong 194
752. Grace Ngu-Aneneba 194
753. Gwen Tanyi 194
754. Margaret Fogam 194
755. RoseMary Ngehsab Lum 195
756. Judith Balon 195
757. Gaël Gbristyles 195
758. Sama Victor Gwanmesia 195
759. Martin Foy 195
760. Momabeatrice's World 195
761. Diane Daiga 195
762. Asseneh Christine Lambou 196
763. Irene Kijem 196
764. Passy Chebe 196
765. Abia Rogers 196
766. Auntiefaus Nimongum 196
767. Ngwa Angeline 196
768. Gakehmi Nadege 196
769. Mathias Fobi 197

770. Loh Benson...197
771. Aneneba Akufor 197
772. Bernadette Tita 197
773. Priscilla Neng Mulesiwi 197
774. Nji Evelyn..197
775. Chesi Miki 197
776. Isabelle Kum Diom..198
777. Roseta Ade...198
778. Bernardine Audrey Yaya Wirnkar 198
779. Mumbali 198
780. Larry Chukwunonso 198
781. Cylvia Tebit...198
782. Eve Mathy 198
783. Evelyn Angu..199
784. Stephen Tanjang 199
785. Gisele Mofor..199
786. Marian Mua 199
787. Ethel Bih..199
788. Ma Neh 199
789. Chia Joan 200
790. Wirsiy Yujika 200
791. Chia Joan 200
792. Akosung Chichi 200
793. Maurice Akwa 200
794. Simon Buh 200

795. Kate Che 201
796. Mawo Regine 201
797. Priscilla Neng Mulesiwi 201
798. Christine Ngangsic 201
799. Samegirl Wambong 201
800. Chi Clement Mekolefagh 201
801. Glory Fontah 202
802. Lidwina Kroll 202
803. Giesel Kemani 202
804. Ngwa Angeline 202
805. Taminang Pierre 202
806. Régine Atangana 202
807. Régine Atangana 202
808. Lea Tukele 203
809. Justine Ma 203
810. Rel Rel 203
811. Cloudatte Akwen 203
812. Veronica Awasom-Ntumazah 203
813. Marie Eben Kanga 204
814. Clotile Monikang 204
815. Rose Mankaa 204
816. Fr. Maurice Akwa 204
817. Viviana Aguii 205
818. Gigi Akwa 205
829. Maggi Akwa 205

820. Damian Tem 205
821. Millbrigg Simon Spencer 206
822. Jevis Mai-Akwa 206
823. Sih Enyowe 206
824. Adel Etia 206
825. Agnes Mbongere 206
826. Priscilla Neng Mulesiwi 206
827. Simon Buh 207
828. Njua Christina 207
829. Yvonne Tum 207
830. Jane Bebs 207
831. Marie Wankah 207
832. Hedrine Tamajong 207
833. Jessie Nchuo 208
834. Nkwain Juliana 208
835. Caroline Tenye 208
836. Duchess K Lira 208
837. Berinyuy Willie Shiyntum 208
838. Francis Bama 208
839. Robert Sears 209
840. Mary Asoh 209
841. Rose Vershiyi 209
842. Ibeanuka Ife Callista Chukwuma 209
843. Lydia Ekeme 209
844. Jane Bebs 210

845. Haoua Bobo 210
846. Horty Bam 210
847. Mawo Regine 210
848. Lidwina Kroll 210
849. Tata Viola 210
850. Joan Ngando 210
851. Hilda Ndumu 211
852. Priscilla Neng Mulesiwi 211
853. Roseline Nasih 211
854. Assumpta Aba 211
855. Régine Atangana 211
856. Kelly Prudence 211
857. Karen Giermek 211
858. Nicolyne Fonjie Idem 212
859. Edwige Nmo 212
860. Nfam Tosam Mukong 212
861. Adèle Essama 212
862. Bernardine Audrey Yaya Wirnkar 212
863. Gillian Kitu Njoka 212
864. Elizabeth Mbayu 213
865. Mimi La Belle 213
866. Ngulefac Fondong 213
867. Gabby M. C. Joseph-Ibe 213
868. Martin Jumbam 213
869. Kel MNnbu 213

870. Pretty Medard 213
871. Marlyse Mbanga 214
872. Julia Lum 214
873. Hedrine Tamajong 214
874. Ndemtchu Solange 214
875. Gertrude Tabuwe Sirri Ngongba 214
876. Magdalene Orock 214
877. Beri Nyuy 214
878. Rose Mezu 215
879. Maurice Akwa 215
880. Fonyam Bertha Ananga 215
881. Bisi Njob 215
882. Paulette Synajie 215
883. Mbunwe Colette 215
884. Gabriel Asaba 216
885. Ngwinui Juliana 216
886. Juliana S Asuku 216
887. Priscilla Neng Mulesiwi 216
888. Jane Bebs 216
889. Electa Nsabin 216
890. Beatrice Fri Bime 216
891. Eunice Gwanmesia 217
892. Boja Elsie Kumbong Uwi 217
893. Paulinus Jua 217
894. Nicolyne Fonjie Idem 217

895. Ngono Marguerite 217
896. Buh Protus Biame 217
879. Maurice Akwa 218
898. Odile-Pauline Bandolo 218
899. Odile-Pauline Bandolo 218
890. Maurice Akwa 218
891. Anne Francis 218
892. Kamdem Njomo 218
893. Yvette Atche 218
894. Cloudatte Akwen 219
895. Bernardine Audrey Yaya Wirnkar 219
896. Asanji Niba 219
897. Kah Rogers 219
898. Régine Atangana 219
899. Maceline MB 219
900. Taniform Taniform 219
901. Ngwa Mary Anne 220
902. Zie Nji Atang 220
903. Kelly Prudence 220
904. Naomi Blessings 220
905. Hedrine Tamajong 220
906. Chia Frederick Yong 220
907. Bibiana Tita 220
908. Shey Don Dubila 221
909. Selamo Rene Suinyuy 221

910. Nini Bih … 221
911. Ntaintain Nyiaseh … 221
912. Delphine Nsen Njukwe … 221
913. Rita Cham … 221
914. Beatrice Tangeh … 221
915. Beatrice Moma … 222
916. Assumpta Aba … 222
917. Paulette Synajie … 222
918. Elias Bisong … 222
919. Agnes Mbongere … 222
920. Gnintedem Hugette Temgoua … 222
921. Angelica Bih … 222
922. Gertrude Tabuwe Sirri Ngongba … 223
923. Evelyn Bah … 223
924. Josephine Niba Awounfac … 223
925. Maurice Akwa … 223
926. Nina Mezu-Nwaba … 224
927. Eveline Ncho … 224
928. Angelica Bih … 224
929. Neba Veritas Ngum … 224
930. Aurel Anglade … 224
931. Ngulefac Fondong … 224
932. RoseMary Ngehsab Lum … 224
933. Paulette Synajie … 225
934. Stella Wanki … 225

935. Marceline Yele 225
936. Vy Mbanwie 225
937. Julius Ngole 225
938. Lucien Enguele Ebogo 226
939. Ethel Chu Buh 226
940. Florence Uche 226
941. Dr-Marcelline Nyambi 226
942. Immaculate Che 226
943. Ewane Mary 226
944. Beri Nyuy 227
945. Anang Gaston Heston 227
956. Bernardine Audrey Yaya Wirnkar 227
947. Roseta Ade 227
948. Mawo Regine 227
949. Grace Fombe 227
950. Asenath Asang 227
951. Anita Tuma 228
952. Priscilla Neng Mulesiwi 228
953. Kelly Prudence 228
954. Natang Yong 228
955. Susan Ndefru 228
956. Odilia Fri Mundi Wankwi 228
957. Millbrigg Simon Spencer 229
958. Jane Bebs 229
959. Philip Ngundam 229

960. Hen Ndatchi Mayikith 229
961. Ndiashea Ngante 229
962. Priscille Mbaka 229
963. Florence Asaah Keng 230
964. John Tchamnda 230
965. Ruth Ndonyi 230
966. Mary Njah Foncham 230
967. Ntaintain Nyiaseh 230
968. Duchess K Lira 230
969. Tita Therese 230
970. Shura F. Ursula 231
971. Bong Akwa 231
972. Bong Akwa 231
973. Julia Buban Ngu 231
974. Cinta Chia 231
975. Therese Mezigue 231
976. Ginny Rauer 231
977. Pamela Tegha 232
978. Edna Fonban 232
979. Zida Mua 232
980. Gladys Aborungong Fonmedig 232
981. Dianga Bridget 232
982. Maggie Nyang 232
983. Kel MNnbu 232
984. Daniel Ache 233

985. Ibeanuka Ife Callista Chukwuma 233

986. Mbeng Anthony 233

987. Pruddy Ghong 233

988. Cho Julius 233

989. Felicitas Ayuk 233

990. Lidwina Kroll 234

991. Afanwi Lum 234

992. Alfred Azongho 234

993. Nicolyne Fonjie Idem 234

994. Mike-Anne Waters 234

995. Grace Ngum Awantu 234

996. Beatrice Fri Bime 234

997. Ntumnafoinkom Patience Sama Ndi 235

998. Chifor Marry 235

999. Jinoh Jamet Banjong 235

1000. Ngwe Clotild 235

1001. Régine Atangana 235

1002. Magdalene Orock 235

1003. Maggie Egbe 236

1004. Gertrude Nkie Atabong 236

1005. Maurice Akwa 236

1006. Elizabeth Elangwe 236

1007. Maurice Akwa 236

1008. Besongha Zembeh 236

1009. Brigitte Ngoyang 237

1010. Erika Indira Zara 237
1011. Eddy Etawo 237
1012. Judith Mboge 237
1013. Lemnyuy Dora 237
1014. Banboye Blandine Bongmoyong 237
1015. Colette Tamangwa 237
1016. Camilla Tamasang 238
1017. Francis Ebeke 238
1018. Mary Florence Chia 238
1019. Ngwinui Juliana 238
1020. La Grace de Dieu 238
1021. Matilda Awah 238
1022. Matilda Awah 238
1023. Njua Christina 239
1024. Whitney Braids Besinga 239
1025. Nkukuma Edjoa 239
1026. Constance Tufon 239
1027. Pius Ayuk Agbor 239
1028. Dogo Bridget 239
1029. Mary Mosoke 239
1030. Winifred Leogaa Fofuleng 240
1031. Bei Adela Kpu 240
1032. Biks Biks 240
1033. Régine Atangana 240
1034. Emannuel Suzan Suzy 240

1035. Nicholine Nchangnwie 240
1036. Therese Binfon 241
1037. Cyril Ngwa 241
1038. Angelica Bih 241
1039. Angelica Bih 241
1040. Chinje Loveline 241
1041. Angelica Bih 241
1042. Angelica Bih 241
1043. Gertrude Tabuwe Sirri Ngongba 242
1044. Angelica Bih 242
1045. Martha Pono 242
1046. Flore Mob 242
1047. Immaculate Che 242
1048. Asenath Asang 242
1049. Bernardine Audrey Yaya Wirnkar 243
1050. Jane Bebs 243
1051. Roseta Ade 243
1052. Emmanuel Moma Kisob 243
1053. Priscilla Neng Mulesiwi 243
1054. Nicolyne Fonjie Idem 243
1055. Duchess K Lira 243
1056. André Nko'o 244
1057. Electa Nsabin 244
1058. Felicitas Ayuk 244
1059. Ewane Mary 244

1060. Nkongho Lucy Enoru 244
1061. Godfred Kah Mbali 244
1062. Chifor Marry 244
1063. Magdalene Orock 245
1064. Gertrude Tabuwe Sirri Ngongba 245
1065. Pruddy Ghong 245
1066. Gladys Ajubese 245
1067. Pamela Tegha 245
1068. Caroline Tenye 245
1069. Scholastic Awala 246
1070. Auntiefaus Nimongum 246
1071. Gertrude Tabuwe Sirri Ngongba 246
1072. Maurice Akwa 246
1073. Chia Joan 246
1074. Jane Bebs 246
1075. Immaculate Che 246
1076. Magdalene Orock 247
1077. Priscilla Neng Mulesiwi 247
1078. Chi Clement Mekolefagh 247
1079. Anna Ngu 247
1080. Emmanuel Moma Kisob 247
1081. Jane Bebs 247
1082. Nfam Tosam Mukong 247
1083. Priscilla Neng Mulesiwi 248
1084. Chia Joan 248

1085. Naomi Blessings 248

1086. Julius Ngole 248

1087. Assumpta Aba 248

1088. Angelica Bih 248

1089. Niba-Ahlijah Meh Niba-Ahlijah 248

1090. Mimi La BelleMaurice Akwa 249

1091. Mbanga Rose 249

1092. Mbanga Rose 249

1093. Assumpta Bourgeois 249

1094. Afanwi Lum 249

1095. Asonglefac Nkemleke 250

1096. Mimi La Belle 250

1097. Eddy Etawo 250

1098. Jean-françois Ebah 250

1099. Leonard Ngumbah 250

1100. Prodencia Asaba 251

1101. Anne Francis 251

1102. Therese Mezigue 251

1103. Bruno Kuumtem 251

1104. Jevis Mai-Akwa 251

1105. Gladys Obale 251

1106. Auntiefaus Nimongum 252

1107. Doc Mafor 252

1108. Manso Arrey 252

1109. Taba Eseme 252

1110. Norbert Kum 252
1111. Gnintedem Hugette Temgoua 252
1112. Lem Ndiangang 253
1113. Clem Eto 253
1114. Electra Ngum 253
1115. Francis Bama 253
1116. Elian Mambo 253
1117. Ngufor Delphine 253
1118. Eric Igwacho 253
1119. Hedrine Tamajong 254
1120. Hassan Augustine Turay 254
1121. Frinwei Achu Njihy 254
1122. Priscilla Neng Mulesiwi 254
1123. Rose Rose 254
1124. Yega Elizabeth 254
1125. Cloudatte Akwen 255
1126. Damian Tem 255
1127. Nju Ghong Mercy Mbong 255
1128. Julet Okafor 255
1129. Elizabeth Wachong 255
1130. Jinoh Jamet Banjong 255
1131. Héritier Polomayo 256
1132. Francis Ebeke 256
1133. Ethel Chu Buh 256
1134. Yvonne Tum 256

1135. Niba-Ahlijah Meh Niba-Ahlijah 256
1136. Bessong Arah 256
1137. Abunaw Patience 257
1138. Oliver Asaah 257
1139. Taniform Taniform 257
1140. Kejetue Perpetua 257
1141. Larrisa Azeteh 257
1142. Sih Enyowe 257
1143. Pamela Mbuh 258
1144. Nkongho Lucy Enoru 258
1145. Irine Ekanjume 258
1146. Nkwa Nih 258
1147. Julius Ngole 258
1148. Brandino Kuwong 258
1149. Loreta Yah 258
1150. Abraham Akih 259
1151. Wallang Ernest 259
1152. Shey Limmy Dubila 259
1153. Fonge Vivian 259
1154. Karin Awa 259
1155. Bernardine Audrey Yaya Wirnkar 259
1156. Banla Euginia 260
1157. Theresia Ngeniform 260
1158. Vita Donvialli 260
1159. Kang Lucia 260

1160. Wirsiy Yujika 260
1161. Kum Edith Ewo 260
1162. Celest Tatung 261
1163. Elizabeth Mbayu 261
1164. Mah Fidelia 261
1165. Ngwen Niba 261
1166. Olachi Joy Mezu-Ndubuisi 261
1167. Ebonlo Grace 261
1168. Assumpta Aba 262
1169. Bertila Kongnyuy 262
1170. Therese Ngoin 262
1171. Therese Ngoin 262
1172. Roseta Ade 262
1173. Agnes Mbongere 262
1174. Patience Ndah 263
1175. George Nchumbonga-Chrysostom Lekelefac 263
1176. Haoua Bobo 263
1177. Taminang Pierre 263
1178. Yvonne Fondufe-Mittendorf 263
1179. Flore Mob 263
1180. Rose Akwo 264
1181. Bih Toyang 264
1182. Yaro Loveline Yula 264
1183. Quinta Sangha 264
1184. Immaculate Che 264

Reverend Father Doctorandus Maurice Akwa: 25th Priestly Anniversary Festschrift (15.11.1997 - 15.11.2022), Volume 1. Edited by Nchumbonga George Lekelefac

1185. Grace Asaba 264
1186. Mod Binam 265
1187. Rita Sondengam-Nyembe 265
1188. Divine Nchamukong 265
1189. Bea Prisca 265
1190. Kiven Louis Ntahtin 265
1191. Neba Veritas Ngum 265
1192. Justina Ngeh 265
1193. Emmanuel Moma Kisob 266
1194. Joahana Mambo Tingem-Locker 266
1195. Bernadette Atanga 266
1196. Rosy Touh 266
1197. Jane Bebs 266
1198. Mispa Nkematabong 266
1199. Zie Nji Atang 267
1200. Gladys Ajubese 267
1201. Terri Bueno 267
1202. Vivian Acha-Morfaw 267
1203. Magdalene Orock 267
1204. Viban Helen 267
1205. Love Teumo 267
1206. Ndum Juliana 268
1207. Love Teumo 268
1208. Mabel Nkembeng 268
1209. Linda Akwa 268

1210. Erika Indira Zara..268
1211. Belinda Chungong 268
1212. Pascal Tantoh..268
1213. Jemimah Chuks..269
1214. Christie Ngale 269
1215. Ojong Roseline Nkongho......................................269
1216. Stella Fru 269
1217. Rita Cham..269
1218. Gus Bessong 269
1219. Mary Takwa...269
1220. Bimenyuy Viban..270
1221. Maggi Akwa 270
1222. Ngwa Angeline..270
1223. Eunice Gwanmesia 270
1224. Anna Ngu..270
1225. Millbrigg Simon Spencer......................................270
1226. Evelyn Angu...271
1227. Armstrong Ikoh Awani 271
1228. Virginie Tashi...271
1229. Seh Gladys..271
1230. Philip Ngundam...271
1231. Marc Ndifor...271
1232. Paulette Synajie 271
1233. Kela Delphine Njike-Tah......................................272
1234. Mawo Regine...272

1235. Endy Madukwe 272
1236. Njua Christina 272
1237. Priscilla Woye 272
1238. Rose Achoh 272
1239. Besongha Zembeh 272
1240. Lucie Ngongbo 273
1241. Edward Cheng 273
1242. Immaculate Chongwain Tedji 273
1243. Caroline Chita 273
1244. Mimi Ambe 273
1245. Ban John Beghabe Blaise 273
1246. Florence Ngundam 274
1247. Esther 274
1248. Kamdem Njomo 274
1249. McLyonga Liwoungwa Mota Wenama 274
1250. Chi Gillian 274
1251. Tanwani Esther 274
1252. Nkwenti Grace Annette 274
1253. Tangka Bongmah 275
1254. Evelyn Bridget 275
1255. Kpah Gregoryachuo 275
1256. Ntaintain Nyiaseh 275
1257. Gwen Tanyi 275
1258. Maurice Akwa 275
1259. Nancy Bruns 275

1260. Clemantine Fonkeng ... 276
1261. Mary Florence Chia ... 276
1262. Chi Clement Mekolefagh ... 276
1263. Mary Chilla ... 276
1264. Mbunwe Colette ... 276
1265. Camilla Tamasang ... 276
1266. Bessem Ojong ... 276
1267. Nkenyi Claris ... 277
1268. Attoh Moutchia ... 277
1269. Eunice Neba Ekani ... 277
1270. Wency Nkem ... 277
1271. Emelda Ngwe ... 277
1272. Kel MNnbu ... 277
1273. Chris Fokumlah ... 277
1274. Claudia Kouamen ... 278
1275. Nicolyne Fonjie Idem ... 278
1276. Maurice Akwa ... 278
1277. Rosimex Ndasi ... 278
1278. Grace Ngum Awantu ... 278
1279. Micheline Mich ... 278
1280. Nange Mary May ... 278
1281. Beatrice Moma ... 279
1282. Roland Patcha ... 279
1283. Glory Udom ... 279
1284. Maurice Akwa ... 279

1285. Marlyse Mbanga 279
1286. Lukong Eunice 279
1287. Clarence Ndangam 279
1288. Jim Fleming 280
1289. Scholastic Awala 280
1290. Julia Buban Ngu 280
1291. Nenge Azefor Njongmeta 280
1292. Colette Tamangwa 280
1293. Sabina Jules 280
1294. Lucille Munchi 281
1295. Lucille Munchi 281
1296. Assoua Emmanuel 281
1297. Ernestine Besong 281
1298. Lydia Ekeme 281
1299. Duchess K Lira 281
1300. Maurice Akwa 281
1301. Duchess K Lira 282
1302. Rose Vershiyi 282
1303. Justine Fomekong Jou 282
1304. Nkamsi Besong 282
1305. Rosemary Niba 282
1306. Asong Amingwa Jude 282
1307. Therese Suiru Marie 282
1308. Oben Afah 283
1309. James Achuo 283

1400. Enow Christain ... 283
1401. Nji Rosaline ... 283
1402. Mbianda Grace ... 283
1403. Zebedee T Yong ... 283
1404. Gertrude Tabuwe Sirri Ngongba ... 283
1405. Azinwi Fuh ... 284
1406. Gladys Lantum Achiri ... 284
1407. Lidwina Kroll ... 284
1408. Joh Cecilia ... 284
1409. Pamela Tegha ... 284
1410. Odilia Mambo Akuma ... 284
1411. Cloudatte Akwen ... 285
1412. Clotilde Ngante ... 285
1413. Laura Ngwana ... 285
1414. Pruddy Ghong ... 285
1415. Florence Uche ... 285
1416. Catherine Atesiri Ambe ... 285
1417. Catherine Atesiri Ambe ... 286
1418. Nfon Maurine ... 286
1419. Ebony Shudelphine ... 286
1420. Jessica Kini ... 286
1421. Mirabel Tandafor ... 286
1422. Juskall Meedocktorr ... 286
1423. Charles Osong ... 286
1424. Martha F. Langdon ... 287

1425. Jesse Chi 287
1426. Adel Etia 287
1427. Dorothy Mensah-Aggrey 287
1428. Caroline Yancy-Anih 287
1429. Odilia Fri Mundi Wankwi 287
1430. Martina Mofoke 288
1431. Betty Etonde 288
1432. Rachel Ojong 288
1433. Elodie A. Tendoh 288
1434. Theresia Fuh-Tabe 288
1435. Tim Finnian 288
1436. Anthony Mboh 289
1437. Gwendoline Atabong Nkumbah 289
1438. Debora Fon-aleh Wilson 289
1439. Galega Kenneth 289
1440. Geraldine Tumenta 289
1441. Geraldine Tumenta 289
1442. Jacqueline Mukala Wainfein 290
1443. Hycentha Lai 290
1444. Eveline Ncho 290
1445. Bih Virgilia 290
1446. Moki Charles Linonge 290
1447. Nibalum Elizabeth 290
1448. Lucien Enguele Ebogo 290
1449. Jane Mobufor 291

1450. Brunhilda Asamba 291
1451. Rose Mary Suh 291
1452. Rose Mary Suh 291
1453. Rose Mezu 291
1454. Rose Mezu 291
1455. Bonaventure Ngu 292
1456. Gabriel Asaba 292
1457. Robert Sears 292
1458. Solange Lomessoas 292
1459. Lionel Ayuk 292
1460. Ngwen Niba 292
1461. Cinta Ngu 292
1462. Winifred Leogaa Fofuleng 293
1463. Frankaline Ley 293

Chapter Three: An encomium to Reverend Father Maurice Akwa, by Nchumbonga George Lekelefac 293

Chapter Four: Pictures of Silver Jubilee Celebration of Fr Maurice Akwa 300

Chapter Six: Pictures of Thanksgiving Mas son the Occasion of 25th Priestly Anniversary of Fr. Maurice Akwa, St Lawrence Church, 6222 Franconia Rd, Alexandria, VA, USA 470

Chapter Seven: Other Pictures of Father Maurice Akwa 516

Chapter Eight: Literary Legacy of Fr. Maurice Akwa: 2022 Daily Biblical Reflections .... **Error! Bookmark not defined.**

THE SOULS OF THE JUST ARE IN THE HANDS OF GOD, 33rd, Saturday in Ordinary Time .... **Error! Bookmark not defined.**

DAY 9 – Saturday November 19th, 2022 , CHRIST THE KING NOVENA .... **Error! Bookmark not defined.**

DAY 8 – Friday November 18th, 2022, CHRIST THE KING NOVENA .... **Error! Bookmark not defined.**

GOD INSPIRES PEACE, LASTING PEACE, 33 Thursday in Ordinary Time .... **Error! Bookmark not defined.**

DAY 7 – Thursday November 17th, 2022, CHRIST THE KING NOVENA .... **Error! Bookmark not defined.**

BEING OPEN AND TRUSTWORTHY BEFORE GOD, 33rd Wednesday in Ordinary Time .... **Error! Bookmark not defined.**

DAY 6 – Wednesday November 16th, 2022, CHRIST THE KING NOVENA .... **Error! Bookmark not defined.**

DAY 5 –Tuesday November 15th, 2022, CHRIST THE KING NOVENA .... **Error! Bookmark not defined.**

OPENING THE SIGHT OF OUR FAITH, 33rd Monday in Ordinary Time .... **Error! Bookmark not defined.**

DAY 4 – Monday November 14th, 2022, CHRIST THE KING NOVENA .... **Error! Bookmark not defined.**

Dedication

This Book is dedicated to Reverend Father Doctorandus Maurice Akwa on the occasion of his 25th Priestly anniversary, (November 15, 1997 – November 15, 2022). That the Lord will continue to bless him with the neccesaary graces to carry out his mission for the next 25 years and many more years. Amen.

Reverend Father Doctorandus Maurice Akwa: 25th Priestly Anniversary Festschrift (15.11.1997 - 15.11.2022), Volume 1. Edited by Nchumbonga George Lekelefac

Good will Message from Bishop Michael Francis Burbidge, Bishop of the Diocese of Arlington, in Virginia, USA

DIOCESE OF ARLINGTON   Office of the Bishop

200 North Glebe Road, Suite 914 • Arlington, Virginia 22203 • Office (703) 841-2511 • Fax (703) 524-5028

November 28, 2022

Reverend Maurice M. Akwa
Saint Lawrence Catholic Church
6222 Franconia Road
Alexandria, VA 22310

Dear Father Akwa,

    I extend congratulations to you on the 25th Anniversary of your Ordination to the Priesthood. I am ever grateful for your fraternal support and for your reflection of priestly joy.

    Your dedicated service to those entrusted to your pastoral care, especially the Cameroon Catholic community in the Diocese of Arlington, is evident and you are continuously mindful of the need to celebrate the diversity within our communities and the unity that is ours as brothers and sisters in Christ. Know of my appreciation for your priestly witness of love for Our Lord Jesus, his universal Church, and all God's people.

    As you celebrate this special occasion, be assured of a special remembrance in my prayers. Through the intercession of Mary, Mother of Priests, may Our Lord Jesus bless you and keep you in His care now and always.

                Fraternally in Christ,

                Most Reverend Michael F. Burbidge
                Bishop of Arlington

Reverend Father Doctorandus Maurice Akwa: 25th Priestly Anniversary Festschrift (15.11.1997 - 15.11.2022), Volume 1. Edited by Nchumbonga George Lekelefac

Bishop Michael Francis Burbidge, bishop of the Diocese of Arlington, in Virginia, USA with Father Maurice Akwa.

Fr. Doctorandus Maurice Akwa with the author, Nchumbonga George Lekelefac

Reverend Father Doctorandus Maurice Akwa: 25th Priestly Anniversary Festschrift (15.11.1997 - 15.11.2022), Volume 1. Edited by Nchumbonga George Lekelefac

Other Books by the Author: Nchumbonga George Lekelefac

1). Proverbs Explained (Collection de 1000 with explanations), Snaap press, Enugu, 2006;

2) . True Friendship, Snaap press, Enugu, 2006;

3). French made Easy Volume I, Snaap Press, Enugu, 2007;

4). Spanish Made Easy Volume I, Snaap Press, Enugu, 2007;

5). 2000 Latin Quotes with Translation, Volumen I, Snaap press, Enugu;

6). Spanish Proverbs with English Translation, Snaap, Enugu;

7). Pastillas de Limoncito Para Hablar la Lengua Inglesa, Imprenta Aries, Xalapa;

8). Pastillas de Limoncito Para Hablar La Lengua Francesa, Imprenta Aries, Xalapa;

9). El Inglés Hecho Muy Fácil, Ciudad de México, 2016;

10). El Francés Hecho Muy Fácil, Ciudad de México, 2016;

11). El Alemán Hecho Muy Fácil, Ciudad de México, 2016;
12). El Portugués Hecho Muy Fácil, Ciudad de México, 2016;

13). Compedium of Modern Languages, Snaap Press, Enugu, 2014;

14). El Italiano Hecho Muy Fácil, Ciudad de México, Ciudad de México, 2016.

15). Speak German with me (For English speakers wishing to speak German), New Evangelisation Research and Ministry printing press, Emene, Nigeria, 2021;

16). Speak French with me (For English speakers wishing to speak French), New Evangelisation Research and Ministry printing press, Emene, Nigeria, 2021;

17). Speak Italian with me (For English speakers wishing to speak Italian), New Evangelisation Research and Ministry printing press, Emene, Nigeria, 2021;

18). Speak Spanish with me (For English speakers wishing to speak Spanish), New Evangelisation Research and Ministry printing press, Emene, Nigeria, 2021;

19). Professor Doctor Bernard Nsokika Fonlon, Crusaded for Sainthood in Cameroon, Africa (1924-1986) Pioneer International Seminarian of Bigard Memorial Seminary, Enugu from Cameroon (1951), Ex-seminarian Par Excellence, Socrates in Cameroon, Genuine Christian in Politics, Life, Works and Enduring Legacies, Volume 1, New Evangelisation Research and Ministry printing press, Emene, Nigeria, 2021;

20). Professor Doctor Bernard Nsokika Fonlon, Crusaded for Sainthood in Cameroon, Africa (1924-1986) Pioneer

International Seminarian of Bigard Memorial Seminary, Enugu from Cameroon (1951), Ex-seminarian Par Excellence, Socrates in Cameroon, Genuine Christian in Politics, Life, Works and Enduring Legacies, Volume 2, New Evangelisation Research and Ministry printing press, Emene, Nigeria, 2021;

21). GOD'S INVISIBLE HAND, THE LIFE AND WORKS OF THE MOST REVEREND JEROME FEUDJIO, FIRST NATIVE AFRICAN BORN BISHOP IN THE UNITED STATES OF AMERICA FROM CAMEROON: "Vivit Christus In Me" (Christ lives in me) Galatian 2:20. Motto of Bishop Jerome Feudjio which expresses the essence of his life as a Christian and as a priest in service to the Body of Christ: "Yet I live, no longer I, but Christ lives in me.").

22) REVEREND FATHER MARTIAL FLODORT OYA, FIRST CAMEROONIAN–BORN PRIEST TO INCARDINATE IN THE ARCHDIOCESE OF GALVESTON-HOUSTON, TEXAS, USA: 10TH PRIESTLY ANNIVERSARY MEMOIR (JANUARY 14, 2012 - JANUARY 14, 2022). "My grace is Sufficient for you..." (2 Cor. 12:9); Motto of Fr Martial Flodort Oya.

23) PA PETER ANU ALEMANJI: RETROSPECTIVE ENDURING LEGACIES, VOLUME 1 (1941-2021): Eminent Treasurer, Renowned Secretary General, Illustrious Treasury Clerk Paperback – Large Print, October 18, 2022, by NCHUMBONGA GEORGE LEKELEFAC (Author)

24) Monsignor Doctor Jervis Kebei Kewi: Thirty Fifth Priestly Anniversary Festschrift From Weh-Wum to the Continents of

the World: With A Goodwill Message ... Africa (The Bulldozer-Pastoral Bishop) Paperback – Large Print, October 31, 2022, by Nchumbonga George Lekelefac (Author).

25) Francis Cardinal Arinze: 90TH Birthday Festschrift: From Eziowelle to the Vatican and the Continents of the World. Life, Works, Teachings, Goodwill Messages, Tributes, and Enduring Legacies, Volume 1, Erudite Pastor of Souls, Preeminent Liturgist and Theologian, Lucid Teacher and Preacher, and Cogent Propagator of the Faith, Edited by Nchumbonga George Lekelefac.

26) Francis Cardinal Arinze: 90TH Birthday Festschrift: From Eziowelle to the Vatican and the Continents of the World. Life, Works, Teachings, Goodwill Messages, Tributes, and Enduring Legacies, Volume II, Erudite Pastor of Souls, Preeminent Liturgist and Theologian, Lucid Teacher and Preacher, and Cogent Propagator of the Faith, Edited by Nchumbonga George Lekelefac.

27) Francis Cardinal Arinze: 90TH Birthday Festschrift: From Eziowelle to the Vatican and the Continents of the World. Life, Works, Teachings, Goodwill Messages, Tributes, and Enduring Legacies, Volume III, Erudite Pastor of Souls, Preeminent Liturgist and Theologian, Lucid Teacher and Preacher, and Cogent Propagator of the Faith, Edited by Nchumbonga George Lekelefac.

28) Francis Cardinal Arinze: 90TH Birthday Festschrift: From Eziowelle to the Vatican and the Continents of the World. Life, Works, Teachings, Goodwill Messages, Tributes, and Enduring

Legacies, Volume III, Erudite Pastor of Souls, Preeminent Liturgist and Theologian, Lucid Teacher and Preacher, and Cogent Propagator of the Faith, Edited by Nchumbonga George Lekelefac.

29) BISHOP ARTHUR NICOLAS TAFOYA: RETROSPECTIVE ENDURING LEGACIES (1933 – 2018), VOLUME 1, First Hispanic Bishop in Colorado, Selfless Pastor with Pastoral Charity and with the Smell of the Sheep, Edited by Nchumbonga George Lekelefac.

30) Reverend Father Doctorandus Maurice Akwa: 25th Priestly Anniversary Festschrift (15.11.1997 - 15.11.2022): From Weh-Wum to Bertoua and the United States of America, Life, Works, Tributes, Good Will Messages, and Immortal Literary Legacies, Volume 1.

31) Reverend Father Doctorandus Maurice Akwa: 25th Priestly Anniversary Festschrift (15.11.1997 - 15.11.2022): From Weh-Wum to Bertoua and the United States of America, Life, Works, Tributes, Good Will Messages, and Immortal Literary Legacies, Volume 2.

32) Reverend Father Doctorandus Maurice Akwa: 25th Priestly Anniversary Festschrift (15.11.1997 - 15.11.2022): From Weh-Wum to Bertoua and the United States of America, Life, Works, Tributes, Good Will Messages, and Immortal Literary Legacies, Volume 3.

33) Reverend Father Doctorandus Maurice Akwa: 25th Priestly Anniversary Festschrift (15.11.1997 - 15.11.2022): From Weh-

Reverend Father Doctorandus Maurice Akwa: 25th Priestly Anniversary Festschrift (15.11.1997 - 15.11.2022), Volume 1. Edited by Nchumbonga George Lekelefac

Wum to Bertoua and the United States of America, Life, Works, Tributes, Good Will Messages, and Immortal Literary Legacies, Volume 4.

34) Reverend Father Doctorandus Maurice Akwa: 25th Priestly Anniversary Festschrift (15.11.1997 - 15.11.2022): From Weh-Wum to Bertoua and the United States of America, Life, Works, Tributes, Good Will Messages, and Immortal Literary Legacies, Volume 5.

Reverend Father Doctorandus Maurice Akwa: 25th Priestly Anniversary Festschrift (15.11.1997 - 15.11.2022), Volume 1. Edited by Nchumbonga George Lekelefac

Introduction

This Festschrift is a result of the open letter "my humble writing self" wrote inviting the friends and well wishers of Reverend Father Maurice Akwa to kindly submit their tributes in honor of his 25th Priestly Anniversary. Below is the letter:

An Open Letter regarding Tributes, Anecdotes and Essays presented to Reverend Father Doctorandus Maurice Akwa in Honour of his 25th years of priestly service in the Catholic Church in the Archdiocese of Bertoua in Cameroon and in the Diocese of Arlington, Virginia, USA [November 15 1997 - November 15, 2022] on the occasion of the forthcoming 25th Priestly Anniversary celebration at The Resurrection Church, Burtonsville, MD, USA on Saturday, November 12, 2022, at 6PM. Written by Nchumbonga George Lekelefac, Doctorandus, University of Münster, Germany, Wednesday, October 14, 2022

Dear friends, family members, former students, and well-wishers of Reverend Father Maurice Akwa

Key Statements

It is with profound joy that we inform you that on Thursday, October 27, 2022, our own Reverend Father Doctorandus Maurice Akwa will be celebrating his 25th years of priestly service in the Catholic Church in Cameroon and the USA.

Rev. Fr. Martial is presently a doctorate student in the USA and at the sametime serving as Parochial Vicar in the Diocese of Arlington, Virginia, USA. He is a Fidei Donum from Bertoua

Archdiocese to the Diocese of Arlington, USA.

Reverend Father Maurice Akwa has been described as a Doctorandus in Pastoral Clinical Psycho-Therapy, illustrious diocesan spiritual director for Catholic Men and Catholic Women's Associations, exemplary Cameroonian ambassador and missionary in the USA, erudite diocesan ecumenical coordinator, well-known chaplain and coordinator of the Association of Widows and Orphans, legendary scripture scholar and lecturer, expert in Pastoral Clinical Psycho-Therapy, talented and gifted musician and singer, celebrated basketball coached, eminent choir conductor, one of the founding fathers of the Cameroon Catholic Community for the Washington DC Metro area (March 2006), highly distinguished dramatist, outstanding playwright, and selfless pastor with the smell of the sheep with an outstanding passion for the sick, underprivileged and the aging.

Introduction

"The Nchumbonga Lekelefac Institute of Research, Documentation, Language and Culture, USA" based in the USA has been bravely enthused and stupendously inspired to take the initiative to assemble and publish a "Festschrift": a collection of writings published in honor of a scholar. In academia, a Festschrift is a book honoring a respected person, especially an academic, and presented during their lifetime. It generally takes the form of an edited volume, containing contributions from the honoree's colleagues, former pupils, and friends. The title of this publication will be: **"Tributes, Anecdotes and Essays presented to Reverend Father Doctorandus Maurice Akwa in Honour of his 25th years of priestly service in the Catholic Church in the Diocese of Buea, Cameroon and in the USA."**

Reverend Father Doctorandus Maurice Akwa: 25th Priestly Anniversary Festschrift (15.11.1997 - 15.11.2022), Volume 1. Edited by Nchumbonga George Lekelefac

Our mission as institute is to: 1) Research and document events and the lives of exemplary individuals in society for posterity to peruse; 2) To foster research, documentation, publishing, languages (translations) and cultures of various continents. This corporation (nonprofit organizations) has a literary purpose which falls under educational purposes.

The institute respectfully invites you to kindly write a tribute, anecdote, or paper honoring our own Reverend Father Maurice Akwa. We will be profoundly grateful if we could receive your tributes, anecdotes or research papers on Reverend Father Maurice Akwa via email (nchumbong@yahoo.com) by **Tuesday, November 1, 2022, before midnight.** The collection will be edited and published by our institute on November 12, 2022, in the USA.

Indeed, God has enabled Reverend Father Maurice Akwa to do so many good things and as the mission of our institute, it is primordial to document them for posterity. Reverend Father Maurice Akwa has been very productive with his life and has been God's instrument to many especially as a priest,

About Reverend Father Maurice Akwa

Rev. Father Maurice Akwa was born in Small Soppo on September 22, 1963. He decided to become a priest on the feast of St Stephen, 26th December 1971, shortly after his 1st Holy Communion.

He has been to Minor seminary, 1978-1983, worked in Sonel Wum, 1983-85, and attended Government High School Wum 1985-87 before going to Bambui 1987.

It is when he was not allowed to return to Bambui after his pastoral year in Small Mankon 1990-1991, during the hot days of SDF that he taught in Sacred Heart College Mankon 1991-

1993 before joining the Archdiocese of Bertoua and sent to do Theology in the Catholic University Yaoundé.

He holds a Bachelor's in Philosophy from St. Thomas Aquinas Major Seminary in Bambui Cameroon (1990), bachelor's in theology from the Catholic University for Central Africa Yaoundé (1996), and STL in Theology specializing in Sacred Scripture from St. Mary's Seminary and University Baltimore (2007). [SLT: Sacrae Theologiae Licentiatus, which translates as "Licentiate of Sacred Theology"] from 2004 – 2007.

Presently, he is on a temporal academic residence in Maryland, completing an online doctorate in Pastoral Clinical Psychotherapy.

He has served as: 1) Secretary for Catholic education for the Ecclesiastical province of Bertoua Cameroon (four dioceses) (1996-1999); 2) Lecturer in the major seminary (1998-2004, 2007-2015); 3) Spiritual director of the seminary (1999-2000); 4) Rector of the Spiritual year (2000-2002); 5) Assistant parish priest (1999-2002); 6) Parish priest (2002-2004).

Among other things, he has been Diocesan Spiritual Director for Catholic Men and Catholic Women's Associations, Diocesan Ecumenical Coordinator as well as leading Chaplain and Coordinator of the Association of Widows and Orphans. He has been a scripture scholar since June 2007 – present, a period of about 14 years 4 months).

His Sunday reflections on Facebook reflect the expertise that he has for scripture. Father Maurice speaks English, French. He is perfectly bilingual. In addition, he also has knowledge on Italian, Spanish and some German.

He has a good knowledge of Hebrew and Greek. He has loved Music all his life, being member of school choirs from primary school to higher education and choir conductor for 18 donkey years.

He coached basketball for two years and was Student University President in the Catholic University Yaoundé 1995/96. He acted drama with the seminary troop and a public theatre club, the Merry Troopers, with Ayah Paul.

He is a founding member of the Cameroon Catholic Community for the Washington DC. As a student at St Mary's seminary in Baltimore 2004-2007, with other ex-seminarians from Bambui in association with close friends, they, including Fr. Maurice Akwa nursed the idea of the creation of a Cameroon Catholic Community for the Washington DC Metro area and this was hatched in March 2006. Since then, the Cameroonians have a wonderful catholic community in Washington.

He is passionate for the sick, underprivileged and the aging. He is a true and genuine pastor who cares for the sheep entrusted to him and those far away.

He is sound in scripture and an exceptional homilist. If you listen to his homilies online, you will be inspired by his soundness of doctrine and teachings. In addition, he is an exceptional speaker who can hold the assembly spellbound for so many hours without then getting bored.

Conclusion

For the expanding grandeur of creation, worlds known and unknown, galaxies beyond galaxies, filling us with awe and challenging our imaginations. Lord God, our hearts are crowded with gratitude as we look forward to celebrating the 25th years of priestly service of Reverend Father Maurice Akwa in the Catholic Church in the Archdiocese of Bertoua, Cameroon and in the Diocese of Arlington, USA, Cameroon. We ardently wait with faith, great joy and eagerness, for we are truly grateful to you, our God, for the gift of Reverend Father Maurice Akwa to us - for the great generosity of Your gifts of Reverend Father Maurice Akwa. As you can see, Reverend Father Maurice Akwa deserves all the encomiums from his outstandingly unflinching, steadfast, selfless, and committed service to the people of God in Bertoua Archdiocese and the United States of America. His life has been a fruitful one and God has done so many good things through him. Indeed, the Lord has enabled Reverend Father Maurice Akwa to go across borders, continents to learn and preach the good news, to preach and give witness to Jesus by his life of principles and discipline, life of prayer and life of a genuine intellectual, selfless pastor of souls and illustrious university lecturer and scripture scholar.

It is my fervent wish that we honor this man of God on his forth coming 25th years of priestly service.

Prayer: Thank you, Lord, for the blessings you have bestowed on Reverend Father Maurice Akwa. You have provided him with abundant blessings more than he could ever have imagined during these 25 years of priestly service. You have surrounded him with people who always look out for me. We are extremely grateful for all of your blessings in his life, Lord. Thank you, Lord. Amen. Thank you in advance for your fraternal cooperation and collaboration.

Humbly, respectfully, devotedly, affectionately, and prayerfully submitted today for publication.

Written by Nchumbonga George Lekelefac, B. Phil. (Mexico), STB. (Roma), JCL/MCL. (Ottawa); Diploma in English, French, Spanish, Italian, Portuguese, German, and Dutch; [Degrees earned in order to serve mankind better and not otherwise]; Doctorandus, Westfälische Wilhelms-Universität,

Reverend Father Doctorandus Maurice Akwa: 25th Priestly Anniversary Festschrift (15.11.1997 - 15.11.2022), Volume 1. Edited by Nchumbonga George Lekelefac

Katholisch Theologische Fakultät, Ökumenisches Institut, Münster, Deutschland, Europe.

My signature: Nchumbonga George Lekelefac
Email: nchumbong@yahoo.com

Chief Executive Officer (CEO) and Founder of the **"Nchumbonga Lekelefac Institute of Research, Documentation, Language and Culture (NLIRDLC), USA.**

This open letter led to the collected of a myriad of tributes which have been assembled in published in various volumes.

Volume 1 of this publication cintaisn the following:

A Dedication, a Good will Message from Bishop Michael Francis Burbidge, bishop of the Diocese of Arlington, in Virginia, USA.

The research work begins with an introduction and follows with 8 chapters as follows:

Chapter One: Biography of Reverend Father Maurice Akwa.

Chapter Two contains one thousand, four hunfred and sixty-three (1463) 25th Anniversary Wishes from Well Wishers and Friends

Chapter Three: An encomium to Reverend Father Maurice Akwa, by Nchumbonga George Lekelefac.

Chapter Four: Pictures of Silver Jubilee Celebration of Fr. Maurice Akwa.

Chapter Six: Pictures of Thanksgiving Mas son the Occasion of 25th Priestly Anniversary of Fr. Maurice Akwa, St Lawrence Church, 6222 Franconia Rd, Alexandria, VA, USA.

Chapter Seven: Other Pictures of Father Maurice Akwa.

It is my most fervent and ardent wish that you may give God the glory after perusing this book and above all, that you may continue to pray for our own Father Maurice Akwa, that the Lord may continue to use him to bear many fruits, fruits that will last. Amen.

Most affectionately, devotedly and respectfully,

Nchumbonga George Lekelefac
CEO/ Founder, Scribe, Freelance Ecclesiastical Journalist of the "Nchumbonga Lekelefac Institute of Research, Documentation, Language and Culture, USA"
Oklahoma City, Oklahoma State, USA
November 21, 2022

Reverend Father Doctorandus Maurice Akwa: 25th Priestly Anniversary Festschrift (15.11.1997 - 15.11.2022), Volume 1. Edited by Nchumbonga George Lekelefac

Chapter One: Biography of Reverend Father Maurice Akwa[1]

Reverend Father Maurice Akwa was born in Weh-Wum in the Northwest Region of Cameroon, but ordained priest for the Archdiocese of Bertoua in the East Region of Cameroon.

He has a first degree in Philosophy and in Theology.

He has a Licentiate in Sacred Theology specializing in Biblical Theology.

He has taught Biblical Theology for 15 years in the Major Seminary in Bertoua.

He has been a priest for 23 years and is now on a temporal academic residence in Maryland, completing an online doctorate in Pastoral Clinical Psychotherapy.

Details:

Fr. Akwa is a Roman Catholic Diocesan priest from Cameroon and holds a bachelor's in philosophy from St. Thomas Aquinas Major Seminary in Bambui Cameroon (1990).

He earned a bachelor's in theology from the Catholic University for Central Africa Yaounde (1996).

STL in Theology specializing in Sacred Scripture from St. Mary's Seminary and University Baltimore (2007). [SLT = Sacrae Theologiae Licentiatus, which translates as "licentiate of sacred theology"]

---

[1] Biography of Rev. Fr. Maurice Akwa, https://www.tasteprogram.com/speaker/akwa-fr-maurice/

He has served as:

Secretary for Catholic education for the Ecclesiastical province of Bertoua Cameroon (four dioceses) (1996-1999).

Lecturer in the major seminary (1998-2004, 2007-2015).

Spiritual director of the seminary (1999-2000).

Rector of the Spiritual year (2000-2002).

Assistant parish priest (1999-2002).

Parish priest (2002-2004).

Among other things, he has been Diocesan Spiritual Director for Catholic Men and Catholic Women's Associations, Diocesan Ecumenical Coordinator as well as leading Chaplain and Coordinator of the Association of Widows and Orphans.

Born in Weh-Wum on September 22, 1963, Father Maurice Akwa decided to become a priest on the feast of St Stephen, 26th December 1971, shortly after his 1st Holy Communion.

He went to Bishop Rogan Minor Seminary from 1978-1983, and later worked in Sonel Wum, 1983-85, and attended Government High School Wum 1985-87 before going to St. Thomas Major Seminary, Bambui, Bamenda, 1987.

It is when he was not allowed to return to Bambui after his

pastoral year in Small Mankon 1990-1991, during the hot days of SDF that he taught in Sacred Heart College Mankon 1991-1993 before joining the Archdiocese of Bertoua and sent to do Theology in the Catholic University Yaounde.

Fr. Maurice Akwa loved Music all his life, being member of school choirs from primary school to higher education and choir conductor for 18 years.

He coached basketball for two years and was Student University President in the Catholic University Yaounde 1995/96.

He acted drama with the seminary troop and a public theatre club, the Merry Troopers, with Ayah Paul.

As a student at St Mary's seminary in Baltimore 2004-2007, with other ex-seminarians from Bambui in association with close friends, they nursed the idea of the creation of a Cameroon Catholic Community for the Washington DC Metro area, and this was hatched in March 2006.

Fr. Maurice Akwa a passion for the sick, underprivileged and the aging.

He is now on a temporal academic residence in Maryland, completing an online doctorate in Pastoral Clinical Psychotherapy.

Chapter Two: 25th Anniversary Wishes from Well Wishers and Friends

1. Agbor Michael Ashu
You are a priest forever in the order of Melchisedek.

2. Gladys Obale
Well done, Father. A long time at the service of God's children. You have been an amazing Shepherd. Will never forgot your remarkable service to the Bertoua population and the Dynamic Ladies in Particular. May God continue to strengthen and keep you, Father.

3. Priscilla Neng Mulesiwi
Congratulations in advance Padre. May God continue to bless and protect you in your service for Him and mankind and add you many more years in His vineyard, in Jesus Christ name, amen.

4. Mbunwe Colette
Great Father Maurice.

5. Natang Yong
May you be blessed forever.

6. Paulette Synajie
Bles you Shalom.

7. Lydia Ekeme
JEREMY 15:16, May HIS WORDS continue in your mouth forever, we thank you dear father for your prayers and support may ALMIGHTY continue to bless you IJMN, AMEN.

8. Jasper Nuh
Congrats and may the Lord continue to bless you with good health as you age with grace in his Vineyard.

9. Auntiefaus Nimongum
Congratulations Father.

10. Alice Suika
God continue to direct you Reverend Father Maurice.

11. Viviana Aguii
Congrats in the Lord's vineyard Father.

12. Lemnyuy Dora
To God be the glory my friend Father.

13. Joh Cecilia

Congratulations "ooooo" father. May the Lord be your strength.

14. Therese Mezigue

Mince le jour de ma naissance quelle coïncidence ?

15. Martin Jumbam

Many more years in the Lord's vineyard. God bless.

16. Kang Lucia

Congratulations! Bless you Father.

17. Hedrine Tamajong

Congratulations Fr. Maurice. We thank God for his grace upon you.

18. Sheila Forbi

Happy Anniversary Father. May God continue to give you the strength to work in His vineyard.

19. Edna Fonban

Congratulation's father.

20. Mvomo Michel

Congratulations Father!!! I can remember this day. It was a wonderful day with grace and joy. May God continue to cover you with his lovely smile.

21. Nathalie Lydienne Mekongo

Joyeux anniversaire sacerdotale mon père. Que Dieu vous donne la forme de continuer son oeuvre. Bonne mârche dans votre sacerdotale.

22. Ntumnafoinkom Patience Sama Ndi

Congratulations Padre.

23. Nkwain Juliana

Congratulation's padre we stay united in prayers, it is well.

24. Yega Elizabeth

Congrats Father.

25. Jinoh Jamet Banjong

HAPPY Silver Jubilee Padre!!! May the Good Lord Give you the Strength, Courage and Wisdom to continue your Service in his Vineyard... Wishing you a great Celebration.

26. Banye Sivla Mary
Congratulations Father.

27. Mvo Prudencia
Congratulations Father. Time well spent in the service of the Lord.

28. Ngekwi Betty
Noted Father.

29. Nju Christopher
Congratulations Father.

30. Millbrigg Simon Spencer
To God be the glory.

31. Brandino Kuwong
Congratulation's father.

32. Colette Mbengon Meboma
We will be there by prayer father. May God continue to bless you!

33. Marceline Yele

Congratulations for your Silver Jubilee in Ministry Father may God take your Ministry to another level, IJN.

34. Florence Uche

To God be the glory. Happy Anniversary Father Maurice and more blessings in good health from God.

35. Ngwa Mary Anne

CONGRATULATIONS FATHER. May God continue to Bless You with Strength in your Innerman, Excellent Health and Divine Direction as you continue to serve Him and humanity, passionately.

36. Banboye Blandine Bongmoyong

Thank You Jesus. Glory and Praises be given to God. Thank you, Mother Mary, for watching over your "little" son always in this missionary Eucharistic journey. Congratulations dear Padre. Wish I could make physically but will he there as always in spirit.

37. Maceline MB

Congratulations Fr Maurice. May God continue to bless and use you as instruments of his works.

38.   Abah Quinta
Congratulations Padre. More more of God's blessings.

39.   Ntonoh Belinda
Congratulations Father many more years may God continue to inspire you as work win him Amen.

40.   Nju Christopher
Sure, if the program will be within my reach Father. Program details awaited.

41.   Debora Ngonbossom Kiringa
Dieu continue de te bénir, padré.

42.   Mbanga Rose
Happy anniversary Fada.

43.   Bernardine Audrey Yaya Wirnkar
Congratulations fada. May God give you good health and the strength to continue working in his vineyard.

44.   Taminang Pierre
Congratulations in advance Reverend Father and I pray that God Almighty shall pilot your Silver Jubilee as a Priest

celebration to success. I welcome your invitation with thanks and look forward to.

45. Elizabeth Mbayu
Congratulations Fada.

46. Nsoseka Loveline Leinyuy
Congratulations Father. More blessings. More blessings and fruitful years to come Father Akwa.

47. Oben Afah
Congratulations more grace to continue working in your father's house.

48. Yvy Bebe Darl
Congratulations Fada Mei.

49. Biddy Kaspa
This is our Shepherd. Your flock celebrates with you. Contact Father Maurice.

50. Jeannette Moubitang
All the glory to our Great Lord. Stay blessed.

51. Agnes Mbongere
Congrats and congratulations Father.

52. Brigitte Ngoyang
Father Maurice Akwa, oh yes father congrats.

53. Lydia Nanga
Congratulation's father.

54. Judith Ngum
Congratulation father.

55. Mimi La Belle
More blessings.

56. Ngulefac Fondong
Congratulations Pere Mau. May God continue to strengthen you as you work in His Vineyard.

57. George Nchumbonga Lekelefac
Congrats in advance.

58. Elizabeth Wachong

Waoh fada, Congratulations fada, much love and more grace.

59. Ebonlo Grace

Congratulation's father. More strength and good health IJMN.

60. George Nchumbonga Lekelefac

Looking forward to the celebration. Ad multos annos.

61. Belinda Chungong

Congratulations fada. May God continue to give you strength as you work in His vineyard.

62. Agem Clement Ebua

Congratulations Father Maurice Akwa.

63. Wendy Ngong

Mighty congrats Fada.

64. Mambo Ngu

Congratulations my personal person.

65. Edith Ngwa
What a run, Fada! You're blessed by the best!

66. Erika Indira Zara
Congrats Fada.

67. Jessie Nchuo
Congratulations father.

68. Rose Vershiyi
Congratulations Father Maurice. May God bless you.

69. Ngwefuni Max Igna
Blessing's father.

70. Wirsiy Yujika
Congratulation's father.

71. Judith Forfir
Congratulations. Fada. Many more years in the Lord's vineyard.

72. Victor Nformi

Congratulation's father, may God continue to protect, guide and direct you in your ministry.

73. Cornelia Echike Kwekam

Happy Anniversary Father will call you.

74. Immaculate Che

Congratulations Papa. Thanks for always being there for us.

75. Ernestine Besong

Congratulations Fada. May the Good Sheppard continue to direct you.

76. Grace Fombe

Congratulations Father Maurice.

77. Simon Nguepi

Congratulations.

78. Cloudatte Akwen

Congratulations Fada. Wishing you many more celebrations.

79. Doris Bei
Congratulations Father, I pray God gives you long life to continue to save in his Vineyard.

80. Florence Asaah Keng
Congratulations fada.

81. Mawo Regine
Wow father, 25 the anniversary loading. Congratulations father.

82. Pammella Ngefor
Congratulations Fada.

83. Odette Mbie
And I remember vivdly that day when I was conducting during the ordination mass in St Martin. Congratulation's father. It's been God all this while.

84. Maurice Akwa
Odette Mbie my eyewitness.

85. Gnintedem Hugette Temgoua
Congratulations Father Maurice.

86. **Duchess K Lira**
The Lord's Chosen One. Happy Anniversary!

87. **Julet Okafor**
Happy anniversary father and more grace.

88. **Jeogras Ntube**
Congrats father.

89. **Raymond Assila**
Congratulations papa for your wander full times you give us. Wishing you more Anniversary papa the best.

90. **Loreta Yah**
Congratulation's father and thanks for the services.

91. **Njua Christina**
Congratulation's father.

92. **Assumpta Aba**
Congratulations Father. May the Almighty God give you

the strength to continue to do His will.

93. Lidwina Kroll

May contain congratulations, celebration, congrats and party.

94. Gilda Ryan Ewang Ngwesse

"Here is my servant whom I uphold, my chosen one in whom my soul delights." Congratulations Padre. I will be your guest!

95. Gus Bessong

Congratulation Fada!

96. Pamela Tegha

Congrats father. How I wish to be there to witness this great event.

97. Caroline Tcheffo

Congratulation's father. Wishing you many more Anniversaries.

98. Mary Mah

Congratulations and Abundant blessings Padre.

99. Racheal Atanga
Congratulations.

100. Mary Njah Foncham
Father, Praise God for the years you have served in His Vineyard.

101. Nicolyne Fonjie Idem
Congratulations Rev Father.

102. Angelica Bih
Congratulations Father.

103. Roseline Nasih
Congratulations father.may the Good Lord continue to bless and protect you as you carry on your priestly duties.

104. Beatrice Moma
Congrats Fada!

105. Bakia Anjie
Congratulations Father!

106. Paul Ken Asobo
Congratulations Fr. Maurice. We join you to thank God for your wonderful work in His Farm. Wish you continued good health and wisdom in the years ahead.

107. Bernice Yong
Congratulations Father May his grace continue to dwell in you.

108. Ncham Emma
Congrats Father and happy anniversary in advance. May our good Lord continue to guard and protect you as you lead His flock.

109. MultiTasker Numéro-Uno
Will be present father.

110. Maurice Akwa
MultiTasker Numéro-Uno great to have you, my missing friend.

111. Martha Ketchu
Congrats father more wisdom.

112. Cho Che Ivo
Father Maurice, happy anniversary in advance.

113. La Grace de Dieu
Congratulations Padre, j y serai par la grace de Dieu.

114. Ibeanuka Ife Callista Chukwuma
Congratulations Padre, happy anniversary and many more in the Lord's.

115. Gwanmesia Pamela Bakoh
Congrats ooo Bah. I remember the 15th at the Major Seminary in Bertoua. God keep you safe in his vineyard.

116. Henry Mua
Congratulations Reverend Father Maurice and to God be the Glory, your family and friends including me, who have been with you throughout your services as a servant of God. I am pleased to testify here that you are a light that shines through the path of darkness.

117. Nkamsi Besong

Happy Silver Jubilee celebration in advance. I am looking forward in joining you during your anniversary mass celebration. Thank God for the continuous graces in your life in God's vineyard. Remain blessed.

118. Hilda Ndumu

United in prayers FADA.

119. Therese Binfon

Amen Papa.

120. Kejetue Perpetua

Christ has made you, His own messenger sending you out into the whole world to preach His own word. Congratulation's father. Its silver let's celebrate.

121. Jane Mobufor

Happy anniversary father Mau, my spiritual director. I am blessed to have you in my life.

122. Catherine Atesiri Ambe

Amen ooooh my great Rev the almighty will continue to shower you with his Blessing.

123. Electa Nsabin
Kodos to you Tachu.

124. Florence Kouchou
Congratulations to you father and more grease to your elbows!

125. Prosper Wang Tih Besibang
OMG.... Not to miss oh.

126. Kongnso Prudencia
Congratulation's father. Let Christ continue to be your role model.

127. Ndum Juliana
Congratulations my father we thank God Almighty for your service in His vineyard.

128. Kintang Dufe
Congratulations father please father also pray for me and my children.

129. Maggie Egbe
Congratulation's mom Padre! Thank you for your

stewardship! Many more blessings.

130. Marie Effa
The road has not been easy, but God has been faithful. Wishing you many more fruitful years in the Lord's vineyard. Congratulations.

131. Gwendoline Atabong Nkumbah
Surely and slowly, time passes so fast, we give God the glory and thanks. We thank him for making you faithful to your calling Father Maurice, you have impacted Gods love and word to many. CONGRATULATIONS Father Maurice. Continue with your act of HUMILITY and many more favors are on your way.

132. Father Maurice Akwa
My 59th birthday is here. I will lift each of you and your families to God in the chalice at Mass this 6.15am Eastern Time in the USA. Thanks for your love and prayers. God bless and protect you. September 21, 2022

133. Caroline Asongwe Cho-Nji
Happy birthday fada Mau.

134. Timkain Shella
Happy birthday Father

135. Love Teumo
HAPPY birthday my very own Father Maurice. May the Good Lord bless your.new age and continue to use you to do. His work did touch the lives of others. Enjoy your day. And stay bless.

136. Juliette Nde
Happy birthday Fada Mau and many more blessed years.

137. Viviana Auguri
Happy birthday Father may God almighty continue to bless you and give you more fruitful years to work in his Vineyard.

138. Ethel Chu Buh
Happy birthday Father Maurice.

139. Gigi Akwa
Happy birthday papa Fada. Here's to an awesome day.

140. Ngwinui Juliana

Happy birthday Father. May God continue to bless and direct you to lead his people to him.

141. Fai Wookitaav

Happy birthday to you.

142. Vera Liku

Happy birthday fada.

143. Bin Alice

Happy birthday my biggest brother and father. Wishing you many more years.

144. Marcelline Foncham

Happy birthday father.

145. Ewane Mary

Happy birthday fada.

146. Marcelline Foncham

Happy birthday to you.

147. Lydia Ekeme
Tooop one my FADA FANTASTIC.

148. Sabina Jules
Happy birthday Father Mau. God's blessings.

149. Nina Mezu-Nwaba
Happy Birthday Father Maurice!! We will lift you up in prayers. May God grant you many more blessed years.

150. Fumbii Caroline Ankiambom Niba
Happy birthday Fr Maurice. May the Lord continue to protect and guard you for us. May he continue to strengthen you to be able to do his Will.

151. Miranda Ikfi
Happy blessed birthday Rev. Maurice.

152. Zou Evelyn
Wishing you a very happy birthday dearest Father Maurice. May be an image of 1 person and text.

153. Divine Nchamukong
Happy birthday Fr Maurice

154. Cloudatte Akwen
May contain happy, birthday, to, you, friend and cake

155. Bame Evelyn
Happy birthday father age with grace

156. Nein Eveline
Good morning father

157. Yaah Maggie Kilo
Happy Birthday Fada wor!! You will live long to enjoy the Gift of God's work!! Many happy returns!

158. Mvo Prudencia
Happy birthday fada. More blessings in Your new age.

159. Ntumnafoinkom Patience Sama Ndi
Happy Birthday Padre.

160. Shura F. Ursula

A Happy and blessed birthday dear Father. May God continue to strengthen you and give you the grace.

161. Julius Ngole

Glorious and Blessed years and celebrations. Happy Birthday Father "Mau"

162. Rose Vershiyi

Happiest birthday Father Maurice. Wishing you many more glorious years as you enter into this new age. May God grant you good health.

163. Julet Okafor

Happy birthday father may God bless you as you are working on your vacation and I thank God for you, happy happy happy birthday father.

164. Ngwa Martin

Happy Birthday, Fr Maurice, and many more years.

165. Kongnso Prudencia

Happy birthday father. May the almighty God continue to give you more grace to serve in his vineyard

166. Jean-françois Ebah

Bonjour grand frère. Joyeux anniversaire. Que Dieu achève en toi ce qu'il a si bien commencé.

167. Mbanga Rose

Happy birthday to you and many more blessings and graces to come

168. Cornelia Echike Kwekam

May God continue for use you Hellep we Fadaaa. Happy birthday.

169. Christie Ngale

Happy birthday Pater. God's blessings always.

170. Ebony Shudelphine

Happy birthday Rev. May the Lord continue to bless and watch over you.

171. Elian Mambo

Happy birthday fada!!!

172. Olachi Joy Mezu-Ndubuisi

Happy Birthday, Father Maurice. Wishing you God's blessings and protection as you continue to shepherd His flock.

173. Victor Nformi

May Go God continue to strengthen you in the ministry, keep you healthy in body and in spirit. Continue to age with grace and wisdom

174. Fonguh Bih

Amen. Thanks Father. HAPPY AND JOYFUL BIRTHDAY.

175. Lawrence Eyabi

Happy birthday fada

176. Kilian Waindim

Happy birthday and abundant blessings Fr.

177. Yaya Yvette

Happy birthday fada. Blessings always.

178. Mvomo Michel

Happy Birthday lovely father. May God bless you and givre all the graces you need.

179. Elizabeth Wachong

Happy birthday fada, many years and God's blessings.

180. Nicolyne Fonjie Idem

Happy birthday Father Maurice.Keep soaring higher with plenty Grace and mercies of GOD.

181. Fille Pygmée Badia

Fada Mau, happy birthday hearts.

182. Michael Mua

Happy birthday Father. May God continue to bless you abundantly today and always

183. Anjifua Ntonghanwah

Happy birthday father.

184. Nkwain Juliana

Happy birthday Fada Maurice. Many years of good health and may the lord give you more wisdom to feed the soul every day as you have been doing. Thank you for all the work you do everyday to improve our love for God.

185. Flore Kabiyene
Happy birthday Father Maurice Akwa.

186. Constance Kemeyong Megouya
Happy birthday Father, may the Lord continue to bless you ans protect you

187. Elodie A. Tendoh
Happy Birthday father, may our good Lord continue to bless you with good health and all that your heart desires

188. Marlyse Mbanga
Happy birthday father. Pluie de benediction

189. Nju Ghong Mercy Mbong
Happy cake day farher enjoy. May your new age remain blessed.

190. Tegha Ajemawen Amaazee
Happy birthday father.

191. Agbor Michael Ashu
Amen Padre

192. Anthony Ateh
I will never stop for a minute from counting my blessings and naming them one by one for all the great things God has done to me through these 59 years of my life. Thanks to Dad and Mom for cooperating with God. Fr. Maurice, happy birthday to us.

193. Millbrigg Simon Spencer
Wishing you a very happy birthday fada Mau

194. Prodencia Asaba
Happy birthday Fr Maurice. May the good Lord continue to guide you for us.

195. Anne Francis
Happiest birthday Father, plenty finer things locate you this new year and beyond. Enjoy good health, peace, love, divine protection, strength as you continuously touch lives around the world.

196. Maceline MB
Wishing you a Happy Birthday.

197. Mbah Rene
Happy Birthday Father. Remain Blessed.

198. Eveline Babah Mbuh
Happy birthday father.

199. Beri Nyuy
Happy birthday Father may God continue to guide and bless you.

200. Lawong Yula
May God bless and keep you now and always Padre.

201. Jane Mobufor
Happy happy birthday Father Maurice, God will continue to guide you and keep you and bless you and watch over you because you watch over his flock. Enjoy your day. Your twin celebration will be in November. I can't wait.

202. Nnang Mathias
Happy birthday Father

203. Priscilla Neng Mulesiwi
Happy birthday Padre Maurice.Age with much grace and more wisdom in the Lord's vineyard

204. Patrick Fohneng Seh
Happy birthday to you Father!

205. Hakeem Noibi
Happy Birthday father.

206. Edna Fonban
Happy birthday father.

207. Patricia Fornishi
Happy birthday fada

208. Daniel Ache
Happy Birthday my dear brother. May God Almighty continue to accompany and bless you in ministering to his people

209. Jevis Mai-Akwa
Happy birthday Padre.

210. Mua Anna Itung
Happy birthday padre. Blessings abound.

211. Maggi Akwa
Happy birthday my PP. Thank God for your new age

212. Abang Emmanuel Toh
Happy Birthday Father. May our Father in heaven continuously preserve you for His vineyard.

213. F Junior Kings
Happy birthday Rev.

214. Vivianne Hortense Matchouanbou
Joyeux anniversaire mon père en ce jour mémorable, que le Seigneur tout Puissant te comble de toutes ses grâces.

215. Cinta Chia
God bless your new age, Father. Happy birthday.

216. Kang Lucia
Happy birthday Fr. Many more blessed years

217. Anne Waindim
Happy birthday Father Maurice. God's abundant blessings on you today and always.

218. Ngufor Delphine
Happy birthday father.

219. Nji Jude
Happy Birthday Father. I pray you continue to age with Grace as you serve in our Lord's vineyard. Amen

220. Emilienne Lavine Lobe
Joyeux anniversaire mon père.

221. Therese Songwoua
Joyeux anniversaire mon père.

222. Eta Oben
Happy birthday Father. Happy birthday to you.

223. Elvire Obame
Joyeux anniversaire mon jumeaux.

224. Careen Nyang
Happy birthday Taachu.

225. Henriette Mengue
Happy birthday Father Maurice and God bless.

226. Gabby M. C. Joseph-Ibe
Happy Birthday to you, Fr. Maurice. May God continue to bless you with good health and protection through Christ our Redeemer. Amen.

227. Regina Tante
FADA. Happy happy birthday.

228. Seh Gladys
Happy birthday Father. May God almighty continue to shower you with more blessings.

229. Celestine Tume
Happy Birthday Fada and many more years.

230. Mbunwe Colette
Happy birthday Fr the Best Age with much Wisdom.God bless your good heart.

231. Jeannette Moubitang
Happy birthday Father. More blessings in Jesus' name.

232. Whitney Braids Besinga
Happy glorious birthday my fada. Many more years.

233. Grace Asaba
Happy birthday Padre, many more blessed years to come. Thanks for all.

234. Mungang Endless
Happy birthday. Wishing you many more years Father.

235. Etty Tams
Happy birthday big bro Father, many more blessings and good health.

236. Patience Enow
Happy birthday, wishing you more glorious years.

237. **Eddy Etawo**
Happy birthday Fr. Maurice. Stay blessed.

238. **Bernardine Audrey Yaya Wirnkar**
Amen.

239. **Banboye Blandine Bongmoyong**
Wow congratulations Padre. Happy birthday father. May Mother Mary continue to be your strength in this missionary journey. Thank you for the prayers.

240. **Duchess K Lira**
Happy birthday fada. Many happy returns.

241. **Larrisa Azeteh**
Happy birthday mon père many more graceful years.

242. **Grace Fombe**
I wish you a happy birthday my dear brother and Spiritual Director. Our God will continue to bless and strengthen you as you serve His people. He is a Faithful God. Enjoy your day Fadamau.

243. Nann Emigold
Happy birthday father and many happy returns.

244. Mbeng Anthony
Happy birthday fr. Many more good things ahead.

245. Dymphna Maybelle S
Happy birthday uncle.

246. Tonain Tonain
Happy birthday to you Padre. Abundant blessings, love, peace and longevity as you shall continue to get stronger in His vineyard.

247. Natang Yong
Happy birthday Fr. Maurice Akwa. Wishing you many more blissful years.

248. James Asonglefac
Happy birthday Fr. Remain blessed.

249. Electra Ngum
Happy birthday Father Maurice many more years. May God continue to strengthen and give you the grace and wisdom

you need to work in his vineyard. I WISH YOU LONG LIFE PROSPERITY AND GOOD HEALTH.

250. **Étoile Du Matin**
Happy birthday Father and many more blessed years.

251. **Karin Awa**
Abundant birthday blessings to you Father.

252. **Peter Suh-Nfor Tangyie**
Happy Happy Happy!!! May our good God who brought you this far, who has the master plan of each life precede each step you take and each message you prepare for His people as the boat steers on!!

253. **Magdalene Orock**
Happy Birthday Fr Mau, Many more Blessings as work in the Lord's Vineyard, age Gracefully.

254. **Colette Mbengon Meboma**
Heureux anniversaire mon père ! Que cette nouvelle année que le Seigneur vous accorde, vous apporte joie, paix, santé et bonheur. Surtout la grâce d'être un serviteur fidèle.

255. Colette Mbengon Meboma
Happy birthday.

256. Kebei Susan
Happy birthday big brother father. Keep on the good work, for the Lord's people love you.

257. Michael Boyo
Happy birthday Father!

258. Immaculate Chongwain Tedji
Happy birthday Fr.

259. Brenda Tang
Happy birthday Padre.

260. Wirsiy Yujika
Happy birthday Father. God's abundance on you as you continue to work in His vineyard.

261. Mbandi Caro
Happy birthday fada. God's blessings. Long life and the peace of the Almighty reign within you.

262. Loreta Yah
Happy birthday father and many more years.

263. Nicoline Chomilo
Happy birthday father. May the Almighty God continue to strengthen you and give you good health all the days of your lifetime. Amen.

264. Ngu Azeh
Happy birthday mon pére. Blessings always.

265. Bong Akwa
Happy birthday Rev. All glory to God for more graceful years.

266. Lidwina Kroll
Happy birthday Padre. More grace, wisdom and abundant blessings.

267. Rosemary Love
Happy birthday father.

268. Nini Bih
Happy birthday father.

269. B-k Marie-Paris
Joyeux anniversaire Papa ! God's blessings, peace, good health and long life fall on you!

270. Jane Bebs
Happy birthday Pater wishing you just what you wish yourself this day.

271. Joy Kahmou
Happy birthday father. All glory to the Almighty God for using you this far. Wish you many more years in Jesus Christ name Amen.

272. Sih Enyowe
Happy birthday Fada Mau. Blessings always.

273. Mike Munro
Deo gratias. Ad multos annos. Ad Majorem Dei Gloriam

274. Darlin Joan
Happy birthday father many more years.

275. Ngwa Angeline
Happy Birthday Fada. Wishing you many more years.

276. Solange Minka
Happy birthday to you Sir.

277. Janet Pfeffer
God's blessings on your special day. Happy Birthday.

278. Buma Wilfred
Happy birthday and wishing you many more years.

279. Fonkenmun Samjella Edwin
Happy Birthday Father.

280. Caroline Tenye
Happy birthday father. May God bless you as you celebrate this great day of yours. May he bring you more joy, happiness and more wisdom as you work in the vineyard of the Lord. Bless day father.

281. Collette Ngante
Happy Birthday Fada Mau my special friend.

282. Neba Veritas Ngum

Happy birthday my papa. May God grant you many more beautiful and happy years ahead.

283. Emmanuel Moma Kisob

Happy birthday Padre. May Our loving God continue to bless you and guide you.

284. Tata Viola

Happy Birthday padre many happy returns.

285. Mac Fornishi

Happy birthday Padre.

286. Angelica Bih

Happy birthday Father. Wishing you many more years in the Lord's vineyard.

287. Pepe Kuchah

Blessings Mon pere. Happy birthday.

288. Rose Mezu

Mon Padre, bon anniversaire, et felicitation !!!

289. Asaba Lylian
Happy birthday father.

290. Kinyuy Nyuysemo
Happy birthday Fr.

291. Pam Pam
Happy birthday father.

292. Chebe Wai
Happy birthday Father. Wishing you all the best in your service to God.

293. Ntaintain Nyiaseh
Happy birthday father.

294. Sheila Forbi
Happy birthday father and wishing you many more years.

295. Nkongho Lucy Enoru
Glorious birthday to you Rev age with grace.

296. Ewee Pamela Zuo
Happy birthday, Father.

297. Nash Nathalia
Happy birthday father and God Bless you.

298. Shey Limmy Dubila
Happy birthday our own venerable fada Mau. Ad Multos Annos. I will give you a birthday shout today.

299. Agnes Mbongere
Happy birthday Father and greetings from here.

300. Ando Casi
Happy birthday father and more blessings.

301. Wallang Ernest
Happy birthday Father.

302. Anang Grace
Happy birthday father. May the Almighty God continue to inspire you to do his work. Age with abundant grace and many more fruitful years, in the name of Jesus.

303. Abah Quinta
HAPPY BIRTHDAY FATHER.

304. Belle Sonkey
Happy birthday big bro father. Wishing you many blissful years to serve the Lord and humanity.

305. Lem Ndiangang
Happy birthday my dear Father Maurice.

306. Ngum Evy
A happy and blessed birthday Fada.

307. Hedrine Tamajong
Happy Birthday to you Fr. Maurice. We thank God for his grace and favor upon you as you celebrate this additional year. May God grant you many more fruitful years as you work in His vineyard. SHALOM.

308. Biks Biks
Blessed birthday FADA, we thank God for the grace of aging.

309. Mbong Mih
Happy birthday Rev many more years of prosperity.

310. Suika Ishatou
Happy birthday dearest Padre.

311. Emilia Nde Ambe-Niba
Happy birthday Fr.

312. Rita Biedenharn
Happy birthday fada. God's abundant blessings always.

313. Daniel Tsague
Mon Révérend, Très cher Frère. En te souhaitant bonne fête à la Saint Maurice, j'y joins mes voeux les meilleurs pour ton anniversaire.

314. Auntiefaus Nimongum
Happy birthday Father, and God's blessings.

315. Netty Ekukole
Happy Birthday, Pate and many more.

316. Juliette Menga
Happy Birthday Fr. Maurice!

317. Marian Mua
Happy Birthday Father Maurice my brother in -law! God's blessings always.

318. Mildrate Nnam
Happy birthday father and many more years in return.

319. Elizabeth Mbayu
Happy Birthday Fada. We thank God for your life. Enjoy your special day.

320. Njua Christina
Happy birthday father abundant blessings on you.

321. Maa Ade Abumbi II
Happy Birthday Fr. Maurice and many blessed and blissful years ahead.

322. Berthe Amboo
Joyeux anniversaire mon père et demeurez sous la protection divine.

323. Francis Ebeke
Happy Birthday.

324. Biddy Kaspa
Wishing you a very happy and blessed birthday Father.

325. Bertila Kongnyuy
Happy happy birthday Father.

326. Mary Asoh
Happy birthday fadaaaaa May God continue to guide and direct every step you take and grant your silent prayers.

327. Francis Ebeke
Yes oooi.

328. Yvonne Fondufe-Mittendorf
Happy birthday Fada.

329. Charlotte Akenji
Happy birthday father.

330. Anna Ngu

Happy Birthday Father Maurice, our one and only State trooper who will jump in the car like a fire fighter and support us wherever we are in time of sorrow and in type of happiness no matter the weather. May God continue to give you that energy.

331. Median Fomonyuy Wirkom

Happy birthday dear Fr. friend! Special blessings from God upon you today and always. Love and prayers.

332. Evelyn Bridget

Happy birthday Father wishing you abundant blessings and many more years.

333. Besongha Zembeh

Glorious birthday father. Wishing you abundant blessings in Jesus' name. Enjoy your special day and blissful years ahead.

334. Oben Afah

Happy happy my father.

335. Mabel Nkembeng
Happy birthday Father!

336. Karen Giermek
Happy Birthday Fada!

337. Magalie Pierre Keil
Happy Birthday Fr Maurice!

338. Alexander Binnyuy Ngalim
Happy birthday Rev., wishing you a blessed day in your new age.

339. Hycentha Lai
Happy birthday father.

340. Brunhilda Asamba
Happy birthday father.

341. Assumpta Aba
Happy birthday Father.

342. Gene Tetuh

Happy glorious birthday Fr Maurice. Many more happy years.

343. Esubat Fonkeng

Happy birthday Fada. God's continous blessings guidance and protection as you step into your new age.

344. Jemimah Chuks

Happy birthday.

345. Ojong Roseline Nkongho

Happy birthday my Rev. May the Lors continue to give you more strength to serve your people in Jesus' name, Amen.

346. Frida Ngu

Happy birthday Father! May the good Lord bless you with tons of blessings and many many more years! Enjoy the day that the Lord reserved just for you!!

347. Augustine Bikim

Happy blessed birthday father

348. Augustine Bikim
Happy birthday.

349. Rosy Touh
Happy and blessed birthday fada.

350. Ngoum Jovita
Happy Birthday fada many more blissful years.

351. Bertha Waindim
Happy blessed birthday Rev.

352. Kel MNnbu
Wishing you a Happy Birthday Fr Maurice.

353. Jemia Asobo A Minang
Happy birthday Father Maurice. May our good Lord continue to pour out His abundant blessings on you.

354. Gus Bessong
Happy birthday Fada!

355. Winifred Leogaa Fofuleng
Happy birthday Pedro. May our good God grant you your heart desires in Jesus Christ mighty name. Amen.

356. Rita N Fang
Happy birthday Father, wishing you long life.

357. Nkukuma Edjoa
Happy birthday.

358. Rita Cham
Happy blessed birthday my father the best. Age with grace and wisdom. May God continue to give you the strength and wisdom to continue to carry on his work. Enjoy your day, wishing you your heart's desires.

359. Yvonne Standley
Happy birthday Fada may God continue to bless you with many more years.

360. Cho Nji Stephen
Fada, Happy Birthday.

361. Ebonlo Grace

Happy birthday father. May Almighty God continue to shower you with his heavenly blessings.

362. Jinoh Jamet Banjong

HAPPY BIRTHDAY PADRE!

363. Sofa Bertila

Happy birthday father.

364. Janice Hoover-Durel

Happy Birthday.

365. Chris Fokumlah

Happy Birthday Father.

366. Pauline Asobo

HAPPY BIRTHDAY Fada. May this additional year shower you with God's abundant blessings.

367. Chimène Nlong

Happy Birthday Father Maurice.

368. Kum Edith Ewo
Happy birthday Father. I wish you many more blissful years.

369. Nicholine Ndikum
Happy birthday to you our one and only Fada Mau. May God's rich favor continue to locate you today and always IJN.

370. Brian H. Reynolds
Happy birthday, Father!

371. Bertrand Tchoumi
Joyeux anniversaire.

372. Viban Helen
Happy birthday to you Fada Maurice. May God continue to bless, protect and guide you all the years of your life. Celebrate Happy Birthday.

373. MC Christabell Tanteh
It's my father in the Lord's birthday. Fada Mau, you already know my love for you. On this day, I wish you nothing but love, peace, great health and long life.

374. Anthonia Chenyi
Happy and blessed birthday Father may God almighty continue to guide and protect you.

375. Roseta Ade
Many more healthy and fruitful years Father Mau.

376. Geraldine Tar
Immense thanks Fr. Happy birthday to you.

377. Ngulefac Fondong
Happy Birthday Pere Mau.

378. Mandy Fonkeng
Happy Birthday.

379. Mary Takwa
Birthday Blessings Fada!

380. Wisdom Elizabeth
Happy birthday father.

381. Kuna Flo
Happy birthday.

382. Mah Fidelia
Happy birthday Father.

383. Ernestine Besong
Many more blessed years Fada.

384. Bei Adela Kpu
Happy birthday Father. May God bless you in your new age.

385. Pride Funju
Happy birthday Rev.

386. Mike-Anne Waters
God's blessings on your birthday, good father.

387. Jacqueline Nju-Ghong
Happy birthday to my very own Fada.

388. Michael Gorman
Birthday blessings, Fr. Maurice!

389. Rachel Ojong
Happy birthday Fada.

390. Margaret Sihmeg
Happy birthday Father Maurice. Aged with Grace. May the Good Lord continue to give you strength as you continue to spread the good news.

391. Adel Etia
Happy Happy Happy Birthday my own Complice to your New age and wishing you Many more healthier Days ahead.

392. Giesel Kemani
Happy birthday father Maurice Akwa.

393. Mbanga Paul Ngwa
Happy birthday Father.

394. Vita Donvialli
Wishing you a very happy birthday Fada Maurice Akwa. Remain blessed in the Lord.

395. Priscilla Woye
Happy birthday Father.

396. Margaret Fogam
Happy birthday Fada. Abundant blessings and God's guidance in your pastoral duties.

397. Apollonia Bongwir
Happy Anniversary Father Mau!
I celebrate with you on This special day.

398. Rose Achoh
Happy birthday Fada Maurice. Many more fruitful years and God's abundant blessings.

399. Patience Mbonifor
Happy Birthday Father Maurice! May God grant you all your heart's desires this year.

400. Ntonoh Belinda
Happy birthday fada.

401. Mimi Ambe

Happy birthday Fr Mau, as you celebrate your birthday, may God's blessings, grace, favor, and guidance continue to be with you.

402. Sina Gbake

Joyeux anniversaries mon père.

403. Erika Indira Zara

Happy Birthday FADA. Enjoy your new age.

404. Gladys Lantum Achiri

Happy Birthday Fada Mau. Wishing you many more blissful years ahead. God's continues blessings and guidance as you lead his flock.

405. Grace Ngum Awantu

Happy birthday Father. Age gracefully.

406. Mispa Lachris

Happy birthday father.

407. Mimi La Belle
Happy birthday fada. Many better years ahead. Stay blessed.

408. Cinta Chia
Happy birthday Father and many more years to celebrate.

409. Mathias Akih
Happy Birthday and many more fruitful years ahead, Revd. Father.

410. Nkenyi Claris
Happy birthday Fada Maurice.

411. Yega Elizabeth
Happy Happy Birthday. May the Almighty God continue to bless and prosper you in everything you do.

412. Swiri Rose Saningong
Happy Birthday, fada. Many more impactful years ahead fada.

413. Helen Tambe
Happy birthday Father.

414. Martha F. Langdon
Happy Birthday!!!!!

415. Niba-Ahlijah Meh Niba-Ahlijah
Happy birthday Tah Father.

416. Betty Schmedes
Happy Birthday Fr. Maurice.

417. Yvonne Nyambi
Happy birthday Father.

418. Hen Ndatchi Mayikith
Happy Birthday father. I pray for you today and ask Our Good God to Bless you abundantly today and for many more years to come. Thank you, father, for your prayers Amen.

419. Ernestine Esambe
Happy birthday Father.

420. Laura Ngwana
Happy birthday Fada. Enjoy your born day.

421. Wan Lii
May God bless you and always keep you strong. Happy Birthday Fr. Mau.

422. Lucille Munchi
Happy birthday padre.

423. Immaculate Che
Happy birthday Papa.

424. Kinyuy Forgwe
Happy birthday Fada, wishing you many more years with happiness God protection and blessings.

425. Kinyuy Forgwe
My Heart Love GIF by LINE FRIENDS.

426. Martina Atabong
Happy birthday.

427. Ban John Beghabe Blaise
Happy birthday to you Padre. May the Good Lord continue to inspire you to deliver more and more souls daily.

428. Stella Fonbod

Happy birthday fada. May the Almighty God watch, protect and keep you safe IJN.

429. Ginny Rauer

Happy happy birthday!!! We thank God for you!

430. Mbonifor Emilia

More fruitful and rewarding years as the Lord leads your path big bro. Happy birthday.

431. Nsoseka Loveline Leinyuy

Happy birthday once more Father. Wishing you abundant blessings and good health as you celebrate your new age.

432. Dominic Forka

Happy birthday Fada.

433. Justine Ma

Happy birthday Fada. May the good God continue to bless you many more years.

434. Rosemary Niba

Happy Birthday Father. Stay blessed.

435. Mirabel Ngum
Happy birthday father.

436. Nkah Leonard
Happy birthday Father Maurice.

437. Mabel Ndum
Happy birthday fada.

438. Marcel Enah
Happy birthday Father.

439. Karen Ali Tayong
Happy birthday Fada. Wishing many years of health and happiness.

440. Gnintedem Hugette Temgoua
Happy birthday to Father.

441. Quinta Sangha
Happy birthday Fada. Wishing u many more returns.

442. Michael C. Yuh
Best wishes Fr Maurice.

443. Mary Florence Chia
Happy birthday Padre. May God continue to guide and protect you always. Enjoy your day and age gracefully.

444. Bessem Ojong
Happy birthday Fada Mau and many more blessed years.

445. Joahana Mambo Tingem-Locker
Happy Birthday Father Maurice.

446. Atumbhai Nain
Happy Blessed Birthday uncle Father Mau.

447. Rosimex Ndasi
Happy birthday Father. May the Good Lord strengthen you each day of this new year as He enfolds you with all the wonderful gifts of the Holy Spirit. Wish you many many more years.

448. Zeel Patel
Happy birthday.

449. Geraldine Tumenta
Happy birthday wishes and happy anniversary.

450. Geraldine Tumenta
Happy birthday, to, you, friend.

451. Geraldine Tumenta
Happy Birthday Father Maurice. Wishing you a wonderful Day with family and Friends. Stay Blessed. Always Manyi Mom and Grandma.

452. Emelda Lipawah Ngwanyia-Anangfack
Happy blessed birthday Father Maurice, many more healthy years will be your portion. God will continue to bless your Ministry. Father, enjoy your special day.

453. Gladys Elad
Happy birthday fada.

454. Gladys Elad
Happy Birthday.

455. Pamela Tegha

Hip hip hooray. Happy birthday and many more fruitful years of more wisdom father. Age with more grace. May God continue to bless and keep you for us. Ameeennnn.Enjoy your day daddy.

456. Eunice Gwanmesia

Happy birthday Father!

457. Caroline Mpako

Happy birthday father muam.

458. Pascal Tantoh

Happy birthday Padre. Wishing you all the best on this special day of your life. To God be the glory, Amen.

459. Julia Buban Ngu

Happy, happy birthday to you a very reliable priest, a son and friend. May God reward you for your services to humanity. Enjoy your 59th birthday.

460. Wiysola Gilly

Father happiest birthday.

461. Naomi Blessings

Amen. Happy Born Day father Maurice. May God continue to increase His Wisdom upon you and give you more Strength to do his job Perfectly in Jesus Name, Amen.

462. Noela Gift

Happy birthday father.

463. Lawrence Yong

Happy Birthday, father. I wish you many more years.

464. Ngulefac Prodencia

Happy birthday father. May this new age bring you lots of blessings and surprises. Good health and above all your hearts desires.

465. Sarah Maier

Happy birthday to you Father Maurice. Many more happy years ahead.

466. Stella Wanki

Fada my personal personal.

467. Gwanmesia Pamela Bakoh

Happy birthday Father. Thanks for sharing your blessings on this special day with us. We look forward to celebrating the diamond jubilee next year by God's grace. Congrats.

468. Mary Chilla

Happy birthday our father. God Almighty will continue to bless you with many more years.

469. Clemantine Fonkeng

Happy birthday father many more years in God's vineyard.

470. Simon Buh

Happy birthday to you Father. May God grant you more wisdom in your new age.

471. Leonie Mpafe Samuto

Happy birthday fada.

472. Mathias Njong

Happy Birthday.

473. Pamela Bah
Happy birthday my beloved Fr Maurice. May our good Lord continue to guide and protect you. Wishing many healthier blessed years. Love you a lot, Father.

474. Pamela Bah
Happy birthday wishes and happy.

475. Cham Odette
Happy birthday fada, wishing you many more years in God's vineyard.

476. Jacqueline Mukala Wainfein
Happy birthday father. God's abundance upon your life.

477. Oliver Asaah
Happy Birthday Father.

478. Tabi Irine
Happy birthday fada.

479. Dominican Monastery Bambui
Happy birthday Fr Akwa. May God grant you many more happy years in his vineyard.

480. Emelda Ngwe
Happy birthday father. Wishing you many more years. Marlise Paula.

481. Erika Wright
Happy birthday and many more.

482. Mbong Marie Kembo
Happy birthday father. Many more years and happiness.

483. Chanty Moore
Happy Happy Birthday fada.

484. Taminang Pierre
Amen.

485. Ndidi Anozie Sr.
Happy birthday Padre! Many more fulfilled years.

486. Marie Wankah
Happy birthday my loving padre. Wishing you lots of blessings.

487. Gisele Mofor
Happy birthday Fada Mau.

488. Nji Rosaline
Happy birthday Fada many more fruitful years.

489. Adèle Essama
Ooh! Happy Birthday Padre. May the good Lord keep you longer on earth and strengthen you more, so you continue to do His work.

490. Beatrice Moma
Happy birthday Fada Maurice and wishing you more grace and good health!

491. Anselm Kebei
Happy birthday uncle.

492. Mbei Bridget
Happy birthday Fada.

493. Ndifor Winifred
Happy birthday.

494. Victorine Ambe Dwamina
Happy Birthday Fada Wishing You Many More Happy Years.

495. Euphemia Mah
Happy birthday father. Many more healthy years.

496. Edward Cheng
Age gracefully Fada. Many more bountifully blessed returns.

497. Stephen Tanjang
More blessings Fr. Maurice.

498. Nenge Azefor Njongmeta
Happy birthday Father.

499. Angie Owih
HAPPY BIRTHDAY FATHER.

500. Cecilia Awasum
Happy birthday my young brother. God be your Guide Always.

501. Asonglefac Nkemleke
Thank you, Father, for the blessings and all you have been doing in the Vineyard. May He continue to bless and keep you as you sow seeds of love and understanding.

502. Felicitas Ayuk
Happy birthday Padre

503. George Nchumbonga-Chrysostom Lekelefac
Dear Fr Maurice, Akwa :1. Happy birthday! Wishing you many more years of longlife, good health, constant joy and happiness, and the realisation of all your dreams and projects.

504. Ewoh Nathalie
Happy birthday Padre, thanks for all your prayers.

505. Odilia Fri Mundi Wankwi
Happy birthday Fr. May the Lord ord continue to bless you and keep you strong enough to carry on your ministry of evangelization to the ends of the world.

506. Kate Ngeloh

Happy birthday Father Maurice may this added bring you more joy and happiness and may God continue to strengthen you as you lead his flock.

507. Nkeng Ajua Alemanji

Happy birthday Fr. May you be blessed. Thanks for your prayers.

508. Gabriel Asaba

Happy happy birthday Padre.

509. Dione Amarantha

Happy blessed birthday father.

510. Dominica Ngante

Happy birthday Father Maurice. Praying for more strength and health as you continue to lead God's children back to him. Enjoy the exciting ventures of your new age.

511. Maurice Akwa

Dominica Ngante my big girl!

512. Pam Miye
Happy birthday Padre.

513. Doc Mafor
More blessings.

514. Lilian Ngwana Banmi
Happy birthday Father Maurice Akwa.

515. Huguette Flore Okole
Happy Birthday ooo padre.

516. Godfred Kah Mbali
Happy Anniversary beloved Padre. Many more amazing years in the Lord's Vineyard.

517. Tim Finnian
Happy birthday Padre.

518. Mambo Ngu
Happy birthday Padre!! Wishing you many more years of good health, wisdom prosperity n above all God's abundant gracia as you continue to work in his vineyard.

519. Belinda Chungong
Happy birthday fada Mau and many Happy returns. Blessings upon Blessings.

520. Laure Amougou
Happy birthday father.

521. Chi Alice
Happy birthday Fada.

522. Ngwa Jude
Amen.

523. Ngwa Jude
Happy birthday Reverend.

524. Yvonne Boma
Happy blessed birthday Padre.

525. Felicia Nyambi
Happy birthday Father Maurice.

526. Sam Brunhilda

Happy birthday Father. May God continue to bless you in his vineyard.

527. Gladys Ntang Vusi

Happy birthday small bro/Father Mau. May God's richest blessings continue to abide with you.

528. Clara Chimasa Kien

But to be late than never happy belated birthday pater may God continue to guide you and give you good health as your shepherd his flock.

529. Lambert Mbom

A very happy birthday to you Fada! I spent the day writing a piece for you.

530. Maurice Akwa

Lambert Mbom oh wao !

531. Ngono Marguerite

Joyeux anniversair Mon pere que Dieu vous benisse

532. Gladys Obale
Happy Birthday Father dearest.

533. Cynthia Norris
Happy birthday. You look great! This assignment seems to be a good match for you. Blessings and prayers.

534. Ernest Yemene
Pluie de bénédiction à toi Father.

535. Monice Roca Ntatin
¡Feliz cumpleaños Padre! St. Padre Pio pray for us.

536. Pierre Magouga Mahele
Happy Birthday.

537. Eveline Mbonifor-Mba
Happy Mighty birthday to my personal Fada. May God continue to Bless and protect you and give you many more wonderful years.

538. Maurice Akwa
Eveline Mbonifor-Mba, amen.

539. Rose Rose

Joyeux anniversaire padre. Que le seigneur te béni abondamment.

540. Mispa Nkematabong

Happy birthday fada. May the Lord continue to protect and guide you for us as always.

541. Wendy Ngong

Happy Birthday Padre. May God continue to bless you.

542. Fuh Doreen Manka

Happy Birthday Father. Wishing you more wisdom and good health.

543. Stella Juo Kum

Happy birthday father may God continue to guide and protect you.

544. Eve Fornishi

Happy Birthday Fr. Mau... Wishing you God's continuous blessings and protection.

545. Julius Tuma
Happy Birthday Father Akwa. May you live a prolonged life. Amen.

546. Pruddy Ghong
Bless you more my bestie. Happy birthday.

547. Priscilla Wankie
Happy birthday Father.

548. Nicole Iknicky
Happy Birthday Son.

549. Paulette Synajie
Happy birthday to you Padre.

550. Hycenta Njua
HAPPY BIRTHDAY MY DEAR FRIEND. God, please bless this your humble working for me.

551. Joh Cecilia
Happy birthday oh father. Many many more years of grace.

552. Missmill Akene
Happy Birthday Rev. Father Maurice. Wishing you many more blessed Years.

553. Ndum Juliana
Happy birthday father may God continue to lead you in His vineyard as you shepherd His flock.

554. Suhtah Bangang
Vater, zum Geburtstag wuensche ich dir viele Gluck.

555. Christine Ngangsic
God bless you, Fada. Happy happy birthday to you.

556. Bridget Beng
Happy Fada and many more years.

557. Evelyn Bah
Happy birthday Fada Maurice, wishing you more wonderful birthdays and God's continues blessings and protection.

558. Massalla Irene
Rev., happy birthday.

559. Ngono Son
May your Lord and give you more years in HIS Vineyard.

560. Gakehmi Florence
Happy birthday Father.

561. Florence Forghab Formum
Abundant blessings and good health in this new age. Happy birthday fada.

562. Chiatoh Collins Songbi
Happy birthday and God bless you more Fada.

563. Richard Fobella
Happy Birthday padre brother!

564. Tonjock Cecil
Happy birthday Rev. father.

565. Clarence Ndangam

Have a very Happy Birthday Fr Maurice Akwa. You are such a blessing, and may you be blessed to have even more as you celebrate this milestone!

566. Zida Mua

Happy Birthday Father Mau and Best wishes too. God Bless your New Age Father.

567. Doris Bei

Happy birthday Father.

568. Bridgette Kangsen

Happy birthday dear brother. May the Light from above continue to shine upon you as you serve our Lord and Savior and taking care of His flock. Many more returns.

569. Juskall Meedocktorr

Happy birthday Father. Wishing you God's continued blessings and guidance in your priestly journey. May your day be filled with lots of joy, love and laughter.

570. Kintang Dufe

Happy birthday father

571. Lady-Cel Cornelia EladLambe
Happy birthday father.

572. Jessie Nchuo
Happy anniversary Rev. father.

573. Cyril Ngwa
Hahaha. See My Man Pa Ambe George. Lovely outfit you guys have.

574. Angelica Bih
You will have it my dear

575. Chinje Loveline
My moyo enjoy go pass.

576. Gertrude Tabuwe Sirri Ngongba
I see you people enjoying the wonderful Jubilee of Rev Maurice Akwa.

577. Angelica Bih
Gertrude Tabuwe Sirri Ngongba yes mum. It was a blast

578. Jack Ballad
Congratulations Pedro. May the Lord give you the wisdom and especially good health to continue to do His work.

579. Electa Nsabin
Your regalia speaks for itself. Wish you well in God's vineyard. HIP HIP.

580. Lucille Munchi
Congratulation's padre

581. Eveline Ncho
Congratulation's father

582. Suika Ishatou
Congratulations Padre

583. Ewarre Vanessa
Happy silver jubilee

584. Régine Atangana
Je vous aime, quelle belle tenue. Wum est aux Etats Unis. Toutes mes félicitations, o.o.o.o.o

585. Loreta Yah
Happy anniversary Fada

586. Chi Gillian
Congratulations once more our Spiritual and prayerful Father. May God continue to use you. Happy anniversary.

587. Ambe Sergius
Happy Silver Jubilee Father Maurice.

588. Mbanga Rose
Congratulations

589. Gertrude Tabuwe Sirri Ngongba
Congratulations, and happy Silver Jubilee Father Maurice.

590. Paulette Synajie
Happy anniversary.

591. Atumbhai Nain
Wow what a wonderful 25th anniversary uncle Fada Mau

592. Ebony Shudelphine
Happy anniversary father

593. Ndeh Lum Eucharia
Congratulations

594. Bernardine Audrey Yaya Wirnkar
It was a groundbreaking event. Congratulations oncemore fada

595. Angelica Bih
Bernardine Audrey Yaya Wirnkar you can say that again sweetheart

596. Magdalene Orock
We celebrate you Fr. Congratulations.

597. Rel Rel
This is a beautiful photo fada. Very colourful.

598. Maggi Akwa
Beautiful and colourful celebration. Congrats Fr Mau.

599. Shura F. Ursula
Congrats Father

600. Che Gillian Mbei
Congrats Rev. Father more grace on your elbow

601. Anselm Kebei
What a beautiful celebration Fr. Congrats uncle.

602. Bernardine Audrey Yaya Wirnkar
A summary of the anniversary in one photo. Congratulations once more fada.

603. Pruddy Ghong
You are a chosen Priest. I am Proud of you. Happy Anniversary my dearest Fada Mau

604. Olachi Joy Mezu-Ndubuisi
Congratulations, Father Maurice. A beautiful and blessed celebration indeed. May God's Grace remain on your ministry.

605. Priscilla Neng Mulesiwi
So beautiful.

606. Eveline Ncho
Congratulations.

607. Tah Claire Bright
Congratulation's father.

608. Asenath Asang
With you in mind, God had a better plan. May the Joy of the Lord be your strength.

609. Gabriel Asaba
Colorful and beautiful.

610. Elizabeth Mbayu
Congratulations Fada.

611. Roseta Ade
Congratulations again Father Maurice. You deserved this. God will continue to bless you with good health.

612. Njua Christina
Congratulation's father.

613. Marlyse Mbanga
It was great.

614. Roseline Nasih
Happy anniversary pater.

615. Rita N Fang
A priest, a man of God, a man of the people. Happy Anniversary Fr Mau

616. Mbanga Rose
Congratulations

617. Rosy Touh
Beautifull celebration. Congratulations Fada.

618. Yvonne Fondufe-Mittendorf
Congratulations Fada.

619. Ibeanuka Ife Callista Chukwuma
Praise and glory be to God for a successful celebration.

620. Jean Pierre Lteif
Congratulations father

621. Eugenie Nkemka
Congratulations fada

622. Mike-Anne Waters
Feel the love, father. I was a witness, and my testimony is true, to the love of the Cameroon Catholic Community for their Fr Maurice!!!! God Bless You and your future ministry as he's has done these first 25 years. May God Bless You Always, Mike, your privileged deacon.

623. Ngulefac Fondong
Congratulations Pere Maurice.

624. Maurine Lukong
Congratulation's father

625. Angelica Bih
Can someone spot me in the crowd? It was come and see oooooo. Father you too ooo much.

626. Laura Ngwana
Wow....it is great...Congratulation's father.

627. RoseMary Ngehsab Lum
Beautiful Beautiful celebration.

628. Eunice Gwanmesia
Congratulations Fada on the celebration of your silver jubilee.

629. Sheila Forbi
Congratulation's father.

630. Rosy Touh
Awesome celebration.

631. Mary Florence Chia
So so beautiful. Was there in spirit. More grease to your elbows

632. Ewane Mary
Congratulations fada

633. Karen Ali Tayong
Congratulations Fada such a beautiful celebration. I was there in spirit

634. Dr-Marcelline Nyambi
Congratulations.

635. Emmanuel Moma Kisob
Congratulations Padre. I pray our Heavenly Father blesses you with many more years serving him and tending to his flock.

636. Aggie Elangwe
Congratulations on your Silver Jubilee Fada!! Beautiful celebration!

637. Clotilde Ngante
Happy anniversary father. Praying for you to have more strength to work in His vineyard.

638. Wisdom Elizabeth
Congratulation's father and happy anniversary

639. E Nah Gwanmesia

I can see and feel the love, support, happiness and blessings that your presence always brings to others in this celebration, Father. May God give strength, courage, wisdom and his unending blessings so that you may continue to do his work. Congratulations Fada.

640. Kela Delphine Njike-Tah
Congratulations Fada

641. Emma Yenla Elame

Congratulations Fada. Just want to thank you for all that you do to the Cameroon Catholic community and to Christians at large. May the Almighty continue to bless and keep you strong to continue this process. Thank You! Thank You!

642. Immaculate Che
Congratulations. Father of the people.

643. Gus Bessong
Congratulations Fada Maurice!

644. Duchess K Lira
Man, na pipo! Congrats fada

645. Victorine Ambe Dwamina
Happy Anniversary Fada

646. Janice Hoover-Durel
Congratulations! Very colorful too.

647. Ethel Bih
Your tribe showed up. Happy Silver Jubilee my Papa. Glad to see the outpour of love and support in your community. A community you have served and continue to selflessly serve. God bless you.

648. Manso Arrey
Ethel Bih The entire Cameroonian community showed up. Every tribe was represented. It was a beautiful occasion.

649. Lucie Ngongbo
Congratulations Fada

650. Beatrice Tangeh
Congratulations Father Maurice. Missed this. Will make it up.

651. Bih Marian
Congratulations fada, indeed the picture says it all.

652. Tanwani Esther
Congratulations Fada. It was a beautiful celebration

653. Angelbert Chikere
We heard and felt the echoes... Maurice Akwa
You are blessing good brother. And the community cannot stop testifying...

654. Assumpta Aba
Congratulations once more Father. You have been a blessing to us. I witnessed a testimony about your works in another congregation. God will continue to give you the strength to do His Will.

655. Timothy Clasen
Awesome Father. You and your Family, to have you with us is such an honor. God is so Good to His Children.

666. Abang Emmanuel Toh
Happy silver jubilee father. The journey for golden jubilee has started.

667. Biddy Kaspa
Beautiful celebration. Contact Fada.

668. Mbei Bridget
Congratulations Fada.

669. Godfred Kah Mbali
It's so Amazing Padre. Your Ministre has impacted the lives many. May the anointing overflow. Happy Anniverary.

670. Maryline Shang Nformi
Beautiful celebration! Congratulations Fr. Maurice

671. Florence Forghab Formum
Happy anniversary fada

672. Nicoline Chomilo
Congratulation's father. Your Heavenly father is proud of you.

673. Ojong Roseline Nkongho
Congratulations my Rev.

674. Paulette Synajie
Congratulations.

675. Fonguh Bih
Waoo. Colorful.

676. Mua Anna Itung
Happy anniversary padre.

677. Caroline Tenye
Congratulations big father on your Silver Jubilee Celebration. We join you in prayers to celebrate this great day of yours with the other priest. Bless day.

678. Fumbii Caroline Ankiambom Niba
WAOW WAOW WAOW WAOW. I CAN FEEL THE STEAM FR MAURICE. PROUD OF YOU FR. MAY THE LORD CONTINUE TO PROTECT AND GUARD YOU AND STRENGTHEN YOU TO BE ABLE TO DO HIS WILL.

679. Gnintedem Hugette Temgoua
Happy anniversary Father you have touched so many lives positively God bless you abundantly.

680. Christie Ngale
Congrats Pater.

681. Mbatsogo Kamte Maureen
Congratulations Fada may God Almighty continue to use you on his vineyard.

682. Gertrude Tabuwe Sirri Ngongba
Congratulations on your Silver Jubilee father Maurice.

683. Lizette Tumasang
Beautiful picture and congratulations on your Silver Jubilee Father. You are blessed.

684. Chiatoh Collins Songbi
Congratulations and bless you more Padre.

685. Grace Ngum Awantu
Congratulations Fada. We pray for more grace from above.

686. Bertila Kongnyuy
Congratulations Father. May the Lord continue to bless you as you serve in his vineyard.

687. Florence Tumasang
Congratulations Father. May the Almighty God continue to inspire u to lead your People.

688. Mathias Njong
Congratulations Fr and may God continue to bless and protect you.

689. Median Fomonyuy Wirkom
Congratulations my dear friend Fr.

690. Yvonne Tum
The ceremony reflects who you are. Congratulations again Padre and happy anniversary.

691. Evelyn Bah
Nice

692. Auntiefaus Nimongum
Beautiful, beautiful to God we give all the glory.

693. Juliana S Asuku
Congratulations Fada.

694. Irene Pechase
Well deserved celebration.

695. Judith Bi Suh
This was a memorable 25th anniversary Padré. Stay blessed.

696. Jocelyn Zinkeng
Congratulations Fr. It was nice to be part of this wonderful celebration.

697. Josephine Niba Awounfac
Congratulations.

698. Josephine Niba Awounfac
We give God all the Glory.

699. Gladys Ntang Vusi
Father Mau, you are eternally blessed and a blessing to millions. Nyingong bwase wuh. Kedzong oooooh. Congratulation's padre.

700. Bernadette Atanga
Happy Anniversary Fr.

701. Gemma Abonge
Congratulations and happy anniversary.

702. Vivian Acha-Morfaw
Huge Congratulations father.

703. Cloudatte Akwen
You both are amazing.

704. Bernardine Audrey Yaya Wirnkar
Lovely.

705. Asanji Niba
Happy anniversary my dear and only father.

706. Kah Rogers
Noble path in life.

707. Régine Atangana
Quelle joie de se sentir aime !!!!

708. Maceline MB
Congratulations on your 25th anniversary in Priesthood Fada. God's abundant blessings.

709. Taniform Taniform
Congratulation father.

710. Ngwa Mary Anne
CONGRATULATIONS FATHER. GOD BLESS YOU.

711. Zie Nji Atang
Congratulations and Happy Anniversary Fada.

712. Kelly Prudence
Congratulation's father.

713. Naomi Blessings
Wow, Congratulation Servant of the Most High on your 25th anniversary in the work of God. May Him continue using you as you accept his call up to date in Jesus Mighty name. More grace.

714. Hedrine Tamajong
Magnifique. God bless you all Fr.

715. Chia Frederick Yong
Happy silver jubilee Father, more grateful moments in the vineyard.

716. Bibiana Tita
You both are awesome. Flawless.

717. Shey Don Dubila
More blessings mon père.

718. Selamo Rene Suinyuy
Happy anniversary once more father.

719. Nini Bih
Happy Aniversary father.

720. Ntaintain Nyiaseh
Happy anniversary father.

721. Delphine Nsen Njukwe
Looking fresh and great.

722. Rita Cham
My fathers the best.

723. Beatrice Tangeh
Brotherly Love.

724. Beatrice Moma
More grace Fada Maurice!

725. Assumpta Aba
Congratulations once more Father.

726. Paulette Synajie
Padre locking fresh.

727. Elias Bisong
So handsome dearest priests of God.

728. Agnes Mbongere
Happy Anniversary.

729. Gnintedem Hugette Temgoua
Happy Anniversary Father.

730. Angelica Bih
The men we are here for.

731. Gertrude Tabuwe Sirri Ngongba
Happy Silver Jubilee father.

732. Evelyn Bah
Happy anniversary Fada Maurice.

733. Josephine Niba Awounfac
Congratulations Pater.

734. Maurice Akwa
Josephine Niba Awounfac sister Joe.

735. Prince Garba Splendor
Happy anniversary my boss.

736. Abram Mario
Happy Anniversary Padre.

737. Pierrot Amougou Zambo
Pa'a mooo... I miss you daddy.

738. Vernyuy Nsaikila Gabriel Alexis
Congratulazioni Fr. Akwa.

739. Etiendem Valentine
Happy Sunday father Maurice.

740. Killeng Styve
Happy Anniversary fr. Maurice

741. Ndemtchu Solange
Congratulations.

742. Rita Biedenharn
Congratulations fada.

743. Priscilla Neng Mulesiwi
Congratulations to Fr Maurice. God has been faithful.

744. Immaculate Che
Priscilla Neng Mulesiwi Amennnnn.

745. Neba Celestine Asombang
Greetings and happy Sunday.

746. Steve Angafor
Neba Celestine Asombang hahahahaa, sure they do Celes!!! That blood runs through.

747. Yvonne Boma
Congratulations Father, God bless you.

748. Irene Kijem
Wey, I miss ooo.

749. Immaculate Che
Irene Kijem yes you miss.

750. Abine Florence Bih
Congratulation's padre.

751. Divine Nchamukong
Congratulations Fr Maurice Akwa on your 25th anniversary. Divine Nchamukong. We at Chatnite Africa thank the organizers of the anniversary of Fr Maurice Akwa in his priestly duties. The massive attendance with people from across the world was no surprise to anyone who knows Fr Maurice. I have never seen a priest everywhere and for everyone.

752. Grace Ngu-Aneneba
Congratulations Fr. Maurice Akwa and happy anniversary.

753. Gwen Tanyi
Congratulations. Amazing. I wish I could have been there. Blessings upon blessings to you Father Maurice Akwa so well deserved.

754. Margaret Fogam
We celebrated Fada Maurice's 15th priestly anniversary in Bertoua Cameroon. Fada celebrated his 20th in the United States. Last night 11/12/2022, I was part of his 25th anniversary celebration in Burtonsville Maryland. Congratulations again Fr. Maurice. God bless.

755. RoseMary Ngehsab Lum
Ni Divine Nchamukong thank you soooooooooooooooo much.

756. Judith Balon
This is beautiful! Thank you so much sir!

757. Gaël Gbristyles
Congratulations Father Maurice Akwa. May the good Lord continue to bless you IJN.

758. Sama Victor Gwanmesia
Congratulations Father.

759. Martin Foy
Congratulations Rev. Father Maurice for your 25th Anniversary celebration.

760. Momabeatrice's World
Congratulations my favorite Fada Maurice! More grace!

761. Diane Daiga
Congratulations Fr. Maurice Akwa! Beautiful ceremony.

762. Asseneh Christine Lambou
Congratulations Father.

763. Irene Kijem
Congratulations Father.

764. Passy Chebe
Congratulations Padre.

765. Abia Rogers
God continues to bless you, Father.

766. Auntiefaus Nimongum
Congratulations Father Maurice, happy anniversary. I am glad to be part of the celebration. Thank you for your service.

767. Ngwa Angeline
Congratulations Father.

768. Gakehmi Nadege
Congratulations Father Maurice Akwa and happy anniversary. May GOD give you more wisdom to lead his missing sheep to him.

769. Mathias Fobi
Congrats Fr. Maurice Akwa.

770. Loh Benson
To God be the Glory. Congratulations Fr. Maurice Akwa.

771. Aneneba Akufor
It was a Great service. Was nice to be part of such a milestone. All the blessings.

772. Bernadette Tita
Congratulations Rev Fr Maurice.

773. Priscilla Neng Mulesiwi
Congratulations to Padre Maurice.

774. Nji Evelyn
Happy anniversary Rev. Dr Maurice. Many thanks to the organisers of ths occasion.

775. Chesi Miki
Congrats Padre.

776. Isabelle Kum Diom
Congratulations Fr Maurice. Thanks for sharing. Greetings to the dynamic Cameroonian community out there

777. Roseta Ade
Sunday greetings from Delaware. Thank you for everything you do to the community.

778. Bernardine Audrey Yaya Wirnkar
Congratulations Fr Maurice.

779. Mumbali
Amen!

780. Larry Chukwunonso
More grace.

781. Cylvia Tebit
AMAZING!! AWESOME!! Big, big Congratulations to Him!!

782. Eve Mathy
Thank you for the live. I couldn't be there.

783. Evelyn Angu
Thanks so much for this beautiful live stream, you did an Awesome job Boss. Armstrong Ikoh Awani. Thank you, Mommy Evelyn Angu.

784. Stephen Tanjang
Happy anniversary Fr Maurice.

785. Gisele Mofor
Happy 25th Anniversary, Father Maurice.

786. Marian Mua
To God be the glory!

787. Ethel Bih
Peace be with you. Amen.

788. Ma Neh
I'm watching from home. Thank you.

789. Chia Joan
Your kind heart is reflected in the celebration of this 25th anniversary. May God continue to use you for the Glory of His name.

790. Wirsiy Yujika
Happy anniversary Father. God's richest blessings.

791. Chia Joan
Your kind heart is reflected in the celebration of this 25th anniversary. May God continue to use you for the Glory of His name.

792. Akosung Chichi
Happy silver Jubilee.

793. Maurice Akwa
Amen, Amen.

794. Simon Buh
Happy celebration.

795. Kate Che
Congrats Rev. father. Wishing you many many more years in your ministry. May the Almighty whom you serve, bless you abundantly. Happy anniversary son of the most high God.

796. Mawo Regine
We thank God for his Grace on you and all the challenge s you have faced and overcome especially the health challenge. More blessings Father.

797. Priscilla Neng Mulesiwi
Congratulations.

798. Christine Ngangsic
It's your big day, Father. I pray for God's guidance and protection on you and all who plan to attend. See you soon!

799. Samegirl Wambong
Happy anniversary Fada Mau.

800. Chi Clement Mekolefagh
Congratulations once more Padre. Happy Silver. To God be the glory.

801. Glory Fontah
Happy happy anniversary Father Maurice.

802. Lidwina Kroll
Congratulations Padre. We thank God the father for all the Glory and adoration for His will upon you to Serve His people

803. Giesel Kemani
Happy 25th year of service father. God's grace is sufficient for you. All the best.

804. Ngwa Angeline
Congratulation Fada and happy Silver Jubilee. May the good Lord bless you with good health. Praise the Lord.

805. Taminang Pierre
Congratulations in advance

806. Régine Atangana
Alléluia.......Amen.......Amen......

807. Régine Atangana
Rev Fr Maurice Akwa, tu es élevé, nous remercions dieu pour ta vie et ton service. Félicitations.

808. Lea Tukele
Happy celebration Father. And may God continue to bless and strengthen you in all areas of your life.

809. Justine Ma
Congratulations fada and happy anniversary. To God be the glory.

810. Rel Rel
Congratulation's fathe

811. Cloudatte Akwen
Amen.

812. Veronica Awasom-Ntumazah
It was a blast to come and see. The only person that can and that pulled the kind of crowd we had at the CCCWDC Burtonsville MD, last night is the one and only Rev. Fr. Maurice Akwa. Fr. Maurice, you are truly the people's priest and a disciple of God.

813. Marie Eben Kanga
Félicitations mon père et soyez béni d'avantage à la suite du Christ.

814. Clotile Monikang
Congratulations and happy anniversary Padre.

815. Rose Mankaa
CONGRATULATIONS Fr.

816. Fr. Maurice Akwa

The day we all waited for is Today. November 12, 2022, before now looked like it would never come. This evening with pomp and pageantry we are celebrating the 25th anniversary of Rev Father Maurice Akwa in the Priesthood. The momentous event will echo around the world thanks to one of the thousands of friends of Father Maurice Akwa, Chatnite Africa. If you cannot make it to the Resurrection Catholic Church Burtonsville Maryland, follow it LIVE on YouTube

www.youtube.com/@chatniteafrica.
On the internet: *www.chatniteafrica.net.*
On Facebook broadcast page: *Chatnite Africa*
or on LinkedIn.
*Time: * 6pm in Washington DC which is 11pm in London and midnight in Cameroon.

If you're watching on YouTube, kindly click on the subscribe button. With your help let's build a powerful Chatnite Africa Community through which Africa's story is told to the world unadulterated. The Programs Dept, Chatnite Africa

817. Viviana Aguii

Waooow Father happy anniversary may you be filled with joy and happiness on this your spacial day. Enjoy love in the Lord's vineyard

818. Gigi Akwa

Happy anniversary FadaMaurice Akwa. God richly bless you darling.

829. Maggi Akwa

Happy anniversary Father Maurice Akwa. Wishing you God's continuous blessings and wisdom

820. Damian Tem

I was present at the Saint Martin de Porres Parish Cérémonial ground in Wum 25 years ago. That day, we felt like in the cathedral seeing for our first time, 2 Archbishops came out in company of all their priests just to make you one of theirs.

821. Millbrigg Simon Spencer
There's joy in my heart and it is flowing like a river. Happy 25th anniversary of your call to sacred orders. I'm joining you to celebrate, not the time but the many souls you have won over to God within these years. I say thank you Lord, for the blessings.

822. Jevis Mai-Akwa
Happy anniversary Padre. Wishing you God's continuous blessings.

823. Sih Enyowe
Happy Anniversary Fada.

824. Adel Etia
Congratulations Complice. Many reasons for celebration and Thanksgiving. The Lord has never abandoned us. He was, has and will always be there.

825. Agnes Mbongere
Happy Annivesary Father. Nice day.

826. Priscilla Neng Mulesiwi
Happy anniversary Padre. May God grant you many more years to continue leading his flock.

827. Simon Buh

Happy anniversary celebration my brother, Father Maurice Akwa. May God continue to grant you strength and wisdom as you cross this important milestone of service in His vineyard

828. Njua Christina

Happy anniversary father. Blessings upon you father.

829. Yvonne Tum

Happy anniversary Padre.

830. Jane Bebs

Happy happy anniversary Pater may God continue to guide, protect, as you work in HIS vineyard IJN amennnnnn.

831. Marie Wankah

Happy anniversary my precious Father. Be filled with joy on this special day.

832. Hedrine Tamajong

Happy Anniversary Fr Maurice.

833. Jessie Nchuo
Happy anniversary father. Enjoy that special God given day.

834. Nkwain Juliana
Happy anniversary padre, more wisdom and grace.

835. Caroline Tenye
Happy Anniversary Father. We celebrate you and the great work you have done in the Vineyard of the Lord. May this day bring you good health, blessings, happiness and more wisdom. Have a bless day.

836. Duchess K Lira
Blessed Anniversary celebration.

837. Berinyuy Willie Shiyntum
Happy, happy, happy and happy jubilee my dear brother. We are proud of you as your classmates. May God richly bless you with good health.

838. Francis Bama
Happy silver anniversary in priesthood my friend. I remember that day at Saint Martin parish Wum and the first

mass at St Jerome Weh like yesterday. God brought you this far, give thanks and praise for his grace. Amen.

839. Robert Sears
Happy Anniversary Fr. Maurice.

840. Mary Asoh
What a wonderful day Fr. May God continue to use you for his purpose.

841. Rose Vershiyi
Happy anniversary Father Maurice. Wishing you a wonderful celebration. May God continue to give you the strength, courage and the grace to do good work in His Vineyard. God bless you abundantly.

842. Ibeanuka Ife Callista Chukwuma
Happy anniversary padre, May the Grace of God continue to strengthen you as you win more souls to God, father you are most blessed, and may the peace of God lead you all the days of your life, through Jesus Christ our Lord and saviour. Amen

843. Lydia Ekeme
Amen FADA. BLESSINGS.

844. Jane Bebs
Praying for you Pater.

845. Haoua Bobo
Amennnn.

846. Horty Bam
Stay blessed father.

847. Mawo Regine
25th anniversary loading. Prayers lets go.

848. Lidwina Kroll
Blessings.

849. Tata Viola
Amennnn.

850. Joan Ngando
Congratulations Fada. God bless.

851. Hilda Ndumu
Hearty congratulations FADA.

852. Priscilla Neng Mulesiwi
Prayers for your 25th anniversary upheld. God is your strength and salvation Padre.

853. Roseline Nasih
Congratulations father.may God continue to bless, protect and direct you as you carry out your priestly duties.

854. Assumpta Aba
Congratulations Father.

855. Régine Atangana
Happy birthday to you, blessing, faith, prosperity, healthing from above, amen, amen, amen.

856. Kelly Prudence
Congratulation's father may continue to bless you abundantly.

857. Karen Giermek
Happy 25th Jubilee!

858. Nicolyne Fonjie Idem
Hearty congratulations Padre.

859. Edwige Nmo
What an unbelievable celebration you had yesterday, Fr. Maurice. Congratulations once more on your 25th Anniversary in Priesthood. The good Lord will continue to bless and guide you.

860. Nfam Tosam Mukong
Congrats Rev and thanks for your selflessness.

861. Adèle Essama
Congrats Padre.

862. Bernardine Audrey Yaya Wirnkar
Congratulations in advance fada.

863. Gillian Kitu Njoka
Congratulations Father.

864. Elizabeth Mbayu
Congratulations Fada.

865. Mimi La Belle
Congratulations fada. More blessings.

866. Ngulefac Fondong
Congrats Pere Mau.

867. Gabby M. C. Joseph-Ibe
Congratulations, Fr. Maurice.

868. Martin Jumbam
Congratulations and many more fruitful years of service in the Lord's vineyard, Padre.

869. Kel MNnbu
Congrats Father.

870. Pretty Medard
Congratulation's pater.

871. Marlyse Mbanga
Congratulations. I will be there.

872. Julia Lum
Congratulations Father.

873. Hedrine Tamajong
Felicitation Monsieur L'ABBE.

874. Ndemtchu Solange
Congratulations Father.

875. Gertrude Tabuwe Sirri Ngongba
Congratulation's father.

876. Magdalene Orock
Congratulations.

877. Beri Nyuy
Congratulations Rev

878. Rose Mezu

I'm write there with you, Padre Maurice for 6th Nov is dies natalis for my Mum +Ezinne Bessie Chiege, while 9th November is actual birthday of my 1st son +Obinna Julian, and and 12 November is my birthday - and which is also your celebration.

879. Maurice Akwa

Rose Mezu special prayers for you and family.

880. Fonyam Bertha Ananga

Congratulations fada. We are praying for you and your ministry.

881. Bisi Njob

Congratulations.

882. Paulette Synajie

Congratulations Padre.

883. Mbunwe Colette

Congratulations Father. We will be together in Spirit.

884. Gabriel Asaba
Congratulations.

885. Ngwinui Juliana
May God continue to direct your steps so that you continue to lead his people to him.

886. Juliana S Asuku
Congratulations Fada!!!

887. Priscilla Neng Mulesiwi
Congratulations in advance fada.

888. Jane Bebs
More more wins Pater. I am praying for you.

889. Electa Nsabin
CONGRATULATIONS TACHU.

890. Beatrice Fri Bime
Congratulations and congratulations Father. God's continuous blessings and grace upon you so you can continue to serve his folk.

891. Eunice Gwanmesia
Congratulations Father!

892. Boja Elsie Kumbong Uwi
Congratulations Father.

893. Paulinus Jua
Toutes mes félicitations Pedro.

894. Nicolyne Fonjie Idem
Big congratulations Padre.

895. Ngono Marguerite
Félicitations mon père que Dieu vous benisse ohhhh, Amen Amen.

896. Buh Protus Biame
I still remember one thing the most amazing offertory procession ever organized and executed by the CWA of the entire St. Martin Parish Wum with some 200 women balancing baskets on their heads of the best the entire St. Martin Parish CWA could offer.

879. Maurice Akwa
Buh Protus Biame it was amazing.

898. Odile-Pauline Bandolo
Mon père invite moi ooo.

899. Odile-Pauline Bandolo
Toutes mes félicitations.

890. Maurice Akwa
Odile-Pauline Bandolo merci Ma Sœur.

891. Anne Francis
Congratulations Father.

892. Kamdem Njomo
Pater accept the love of my family as you celebrate this milestone event.

893. Yvette Atche
Felicitations Father Maurice...pour les noces d argent...Reste et demwiee un prêtre selon le coeir de Dieu.

894. Cloudatte Akwen
You both are amazing.

895. Bernardine Audrey Yaya Wirnkar
Lovely.

896. Asanji Niba
Happy anniversary my dear and only father.

897. Kah Rogers
Noble path in life.

898. Régine Atangana
Quelle joie de se sentir aime !!!!

899. Maceline MB
Congratulations on your 25th anniversary in Priesthood Fada. God's abundant blessings.

900. Taniform Taniform
Congratulation father.

901. Ngwa Mary Anne
CONGRATULATIONS FATHER. GOD BLESS YOU.

902. Zie Nji Atang
Congratulations and Happy Anniversary Fada.

903. Kelly Prudence
Congratulation's father.

904. Naomi Blessings
Wow, Congratulation Servant of the Most High on your 25th anniversary in the work of God. May Him continue using you as you accept his call up to date in Jesus Mighty name. More grace.

905. Hedrine Tamajong
Magnifique. God bless you all Fr.

906. Chia Frederick Yong
Happy silver jubilee Father, more grateful moments in the vineyard.

907. Bibiana Tita
You both are awesome. Flawless.

908. Shey Don Dubila
More blessings mon père.

909. Selamo Rene Suinyuy
Happy anniversary once more father.

910. Nini Bih
Happy Aniversary father.

911. Ntaintain Nyiaseh
Happy anniversary father.

912. Delphine Nsen Njukwe
Looking fresh and great.

913. Rita Cham
My fathers the best.

914. Beatrice Tangeh
Brotherly Love.

915. Beatrice Moma
More grace Fada Maurice!

916. Assumpta Aba
Congratulations once more Father.

917. Paulette Synajie
Padre locking fresh.

918. Elias Bisong
So handsome Dearest Priests of God.

919. Agnes Mbongere
Happy Anniversary.

920. Gnintedem Hugette Temgoua
Happy Anniversary Father.

921. Angelica Bih
The men we are here for.

922. Gertrude Tabuwe Sirri Ngongba
Happy Silver Jubilee father.

923. Evelyn Bah
Happy anniversary Fada Maurice.

924. Josephine Niba Awounfac
Congratulations Pater. Blessings for your ordination anniversary. Silver Jubilee is a significant event in the life of a minister of the Gospel. Yours has been marked with untold joys of fulfillment. As you have been much appreciated by parishioners and students alike, the few sad moments of sickness and grief are overcome by the healing mercies of our Lord. Helen and I pray for you to Begin the next lap with spiritual strength and humane mindfulness. Joyful jubilee to you Reverend.

925. Maurice Akwa
Daddy, Rev Joe Set Aji-Mvo, this is paternally very encouraging and nourishing. Thank you for your love and encouragements with Mama Helen Dilys Aji-Mvo. I celebrate a Jubilee of Thanksgiving for God's merciful love with your blessings. I am obligated to you. Rest assured of my filial love and affection.

926. Nina Mezu-Nwaba
Congratulations Father Maurice Akwa!! This is your month of celebration!

927. Eveline Ncho
Congratulations again

928. Angelica Bih
Congratulations again Father.

929. Neba Veritas Ngum
Happy anniversary my papa

930. Aurel Anglade
Congratulations and Happy Anniversary...Father Maurice Akwa.

931. Ngulefac Fondong
Congratulation and Happy Anniversary to you Pere Mau.

932. RoseMary Ngehsab Lum
Congratulations Fada Maurice Akwa

933. Paulette Synajie
Happy birthday to Padre
Happy Birthday GIF by Babybluecat

934. Stella Wanki
Antworten4 Tage
Stella Wanki

935. Marceline Yele
Congratulations Father. Happy Anniversary and May God lift you up for greater kingdom impact

936. Vy Mbanwie
Congratulations Father and May Yahweh continue to lead you in service

937. Julius Ngole
Happy 25th Anniversary of Priesthood Services!! Many more Glorious and Blessed years and celebrations are yours. Thanks for always serving families, friends, and the community.

938. Lucien Enguele Ebogo
Joyeux anniversaire anniversaire d'ordination mon père. Que le Seigneur Dieu Tout Puissant continue à te bénisse pour d'autres 25 années. Gloire à Dieu.

939. Ethel Chu Buh
Congratulations Fr Mau
May God continue to bless, guide and protect you. Love and prayers from your flower girl

940. Florence Uche
Congratulations to you Father. More opening and wisdom in good health

941. Dr-Marcelline Nyambi
Congratulations

942. Immaculate Che
Congratulations

943. Ewane Mary
Happy anniversary fada may Almighty God continue to protect and guide you as you work in his vineyard winning souls, you are blessed fada enjoy your day.

944. Beri Nyuy
congrats father.

945. Anang Gaston Heston
Congratulations and Happy Anniversary to you Father

956. Bernardine Audrey Yaya Wirnkar
Congratulations fada

947. Roseta Ade
With you in spirit Father. Congratulations again. Wishing you good health and many mire years in the priesthood.

948. Mawo Regine
Happy Ordination anniversary Father. We keep praying for God's continuous blessings on you

949. Grace Fombe
Congratulations Father

950. Asenath Asang
You must go with God to any length. Keep doing your work to the Glory of God and the service of his people. Jesus walks with

you everyday of your life. Happy anniversary of shepherding God's flock.

951. Anita Tuma
A very big congratulation's father and more blessed years.

952. Priscilla Neng Mulesiwi
Congratulations.

953. Kelly Prudence
I will be there in the spirit, congrats.

954. Natang Yong
Happy silver jubilee Fr. Maurice Akwa more blessings.

955. Susan Ndefru
Praying for you Father. Congratulations.

956. Odilia Fri Mundi Wankwi
Congratulations

957. Millbrigg Simon Spencer
Praying for more grace to persevere as you continue to minister at the service of God.

958. Jane Bebs
Happy happy anniversary Pater. Praying for God's Divine Intervention upon your life as you continue to serve in HIS vineyard. Enjoy your day and continue to shine in the Lord

959. Philip Ngundam
Congratulations again my brother! May the light of God continue to brighten your path forever, in ministry and in life

960. Hen Ndatchi Mayikith
Congratulations fada Maurice and long life to you our humble servant of God.

961. Ndiashea Ngante
May God continue to richly bless you

962. Priscille Mbaka
Happy blessed 25th anniversary. May the Good Lord grant you 25+ more.

963. Florence Asaah Keng
Whaoooo fada time waits for no one. Congratulations

964. John Tchamnda
CONGRATULATIONS, my dear brother, wishing you many more years

965. Ruth Ndonyi
Congratulations Father.

966. Mary Njah Foncham
Congratulations as you continue to serve in God's Vineyard, Fada.

967. Ntaintain Nyiaseh
More Grace, father.

968. Duchess K Lira
Blessings upon u, Fada

969. Tita Therese
Congratulations Fr and many more years to work in the Lord s vineyard.

970. Shura F. Ursula
Praying for you.

971. Bong Akwa
Happy anniversary Rev.

972. Bong Akwa
More grace.

973. Julia Buban Ngu
Big, big Congratulations fada.

974. Cinta Chia
Congratulations Fr.

975. Therese Mezigue
Happy birthday à nous deux c'est mon anniversaire de naissance

976. Ginny Rauer
God bless you!

977. Pamela Tegha
Congrats oncemore father. Many more fruitful years and blessings in the Lord's vineyard.

978. Edna Fonban
Congratulations Father.many more years in the vineyard.

979. Zida Mua
Happy Blessed 25th Anniversary Father and God Continues guardians and Protection.

980. Gladys Aborungong Fonmedig
Congratulations Father.

981. Dianga Bridget
Congratulations Happy Anniversary Fada. May the Lord Continue to guide and protect you.

982. Maggie Nyang
Congratulations Taachu.

983. Kel MNnbu
Huge congrats Father Maurice.

984. Daniel Ache

Hello, my dear Brother Fr Maurice Akwa, may I avail myself of this opportunity to heartily wish you All the Best in your ministry to God's people. Congratulations and happy 25th anniversary.

985. Ibeanuka Ife Callista Chukwuma

congratulations my father, more years of service in the Lord's vineyard.

986. Mbeng Anthony

Happy anniversary padre.

987. Pruddy Ghong

Will be there in spirit.

988. Cho Julius

Happy anniversary Fada.

989. Felicitas Ayuk

We shall be there by God's special grace. Congrats again. May God continue to watch your steps

990. Lidwina Kroll
We praise God our everlasting father for this 25years of Grace. wisdom and annointing in His vineyard. Congratulations Padre All Glory and adoration to God the father.

991. Afanwi Lum
Congratulations Father

992. Alfred Azongho
May Our good Lord continue to strengthen your sheperdship in His Vineyard.

993. Nicolyne Fonjie Idem
Massive Congratulations the People.s priest

994. Mike-Anne Waters
Happy 25th anniversary of your ordination, good priest!

995. Grace Ngum Awantu
Congratulations Fada. May our good God grant you many more happy years as you serve in his vineyard.

996. Beatrice Fri Bime
Congratulations Fada. May God continue to bless you abundantly and give you the strength to shepherd his folk.

997. Ntumnafoinkom Patience Sama Ndi
Congrats Padre! More grace loading IJN

998. Chifor Marry
Happy anniversary Padre and may God continue to fill you with his wisdom, good health, blessings and many more years in his vineyard.

999. Jinoh Jamet Banjong
BIG CONGRATULATIONS and HAPPY 25th ANNIVERSARY to you Dear Reverend Father Maurice Akwa !!! I wish you all the best Ahead as you continue on your amazing journey of service in the vineyard of the Lord.
More Grace, Strength, wisdom, good health.

1000. Ngwe Clotild
Happy anniversary Father.

1001. Régine Atangana
Toutes mes félicitations, mon père, nous sommes de tout coeur avec toi......

1002. Magdalene Orock
Congratulations.

1003. Maggie Egbe
Congratulation's congratulations Padre! Wishing you the best of luck ahead as you continuously blessed others with your stewardship.

1004. Gertrude Nkie Atabong
Congratulation, Many more successful years of priesthood.

1005. Maurice Akwa
Gertrude Nkie Atabong amen. Thank you very much.

1006. Elizabeth Elangwe
Congratulations Father. May God continue to bless you, grant you good health and more years to work in His vineyard.

1007. Maurice Akwa
Elizabeth Elangwe thank you mom.

1008. Besongha Zembeh
Congratulations fada. Happy 25th anniversary and may the almighty God continue to fill you with abundant blessings, good health and many more years in the priesthood.

1009. Brigitte Ngoyang
Congrats father.

1010. Erika Indira Zara
Congrats Fada. Blessed and highly favoured

1011. Eddy Etawo
Gorgeous.

1012. Judith Mboge
Congratulations Father.

1013. Lemnyuy Dora
Congratulation's father.

1014. Banboye Blandine Bongmoyong
Congratulations to you padre.

1015. Colette Tamangwa
Congratulations Father.

1016. Camilla Tamasang
Congratulations, father

1017. Francis Ebeke
Joyeux anniversaire padre et union de prière.

1018. Mary Florence Chia
Congratulations Father.

1019. Ngwinui Juliana
Congrats Fr. May God continue to bless and keep you as you win more souls for him.

1020. La Grace de Dieu
Padre désolée je suis à Abidjan depuis mardi matin. Enjoy your day, Padre.

1021. Matilda Awah
A mighty Congratulation to You father. I was there when u stated the beautiful race. Can't wait to give you ur flowers cause u so deserve it in Jesus Mighty name. Wish u gd health.

1022. Matilda Awah
Maurice Akwa, I know ...but with you in my spirit.

1023. Njua Christina
Congratulation's father.

1024. Whitney Braids Besinga
Congratulation my fada. You are blessed beyond human understanding. Many more anniversaries in Jesus' mighty.

1025. Nkukuma Edjoa
Congratulations Padre. Blessings.

1026. Constance Tufon
Congratulation's father

1027. Pius Ayuk Agbor
We shall be there come the 25th. May the almighty shower you with abundant blessings.

1028. Dogo Bridget
Congratulations fada.

1029. Mary Mosoke
Happy 25th anniversary.

1030. Winifred Leogaa Fofuleng
Happy anniversary. Fr Akwa Maurice. The Lord is your Strength.

1031. Bei Adela Kpu
Congrats Father may the good Lord continue to guide and protect you as you work in his vineyard.

1032. Biks Biks
Move on in faith, the lord is your strength. Happy anniversary.

1033. Régine Atangana
Mithy father, may God bless you.

1034. Emannuel Suzan Suzy
Happy anniversary Fr. Maurice. May the oil on your head never run dry.

1035. Nicholine Nchangnwie
Wow happy anniversary father and may the almighty continue to strengthen you while we await the Golden jubilee.

1036. Therese Binfon
Congratulations Father Mau. We appreciate you and we love you, Papa. Wishing you many more blessed years of service at the vineyard of our Lord Almighty Jesus Christ.

1037. Cyril Ngwa
Hahaha. See My Man Pa Ambe George. Lovely outfit you guys have. I need my own that material.

1038. Angelica Bih
Cyril Ngwa Hahaha.

1039. Angelica Bih
You will have it my dear.

1040. Chinje Loveline
My moyo enjoy go pass.

1041. Angelica Bih
Chinje Loveline, I tell you.

1042. Angelica Bih
Hahaha

1043. Gertrude Tabuwe Sirri Ngongba
I see you people enjoying the wonderful Jubilee of Rev Maurice Akwa.

1044. Angelica Bih
Gertrude Tabuwe Sirri Ngongba yes mum. It was a blast

1045. Martha Pono
Congratulations oh Father Pa Mau. May The Lord continue to sustain you in His vineyard.

1046. Flore Mob
Congratulations to the people's fada.

1047. Immaculate Che
That's awesome! Congratulations!

1048. Asenath Asang
Beautiful day. It was the day the God made, we rejoiced, and we were glad in it. May your light so shine before men so they may see your good works and continue to Glorify our father in heaven.

1049. Bernardine Audrey Yaya Wirnkar
That's awesome! Congratulations!

1050. Jane Bebs
Wow! That's awesome, congratulations to you Pater wishing you many more beautiful years filled with happiness in your life. stay safe in God's vineyard.

1051. Roseta Ade
That's awesome! Congratulations! and happy feast of Christ the King.

1052. Emmanuel Moma Kisob
To God be the Glory. For 25 years you have been serving our wonderful God. May he continue to bless and guide.

1053. Priscilla Neng Mulesiwi
That's awesome! Congratulations and more grace Padre

1054. Nicolyne Fonjie Idem
Congratulations Fada

1055. Duchess K Lira
Awesome!

1056. André Nko'o
Congratulations grand frère.

1057. Electa Nsabin
Wonderfully celebrated. Congratulations Father.

1058. Felicitas Ayuk
Congratulations.

1059. Ewane Mary
Congratulations fada.

1060. Nkongho Lucy Enoru
Awesome congratulations.

1061. Godfred Kah Mbali
Glorious, thanking God for you and Your Ministry piercing through souls and Nations. Congratulations Padre. Our joy can't be measured.

1062. Chifor Marry
Awesome Fr more grace

1063. Magdalene Orock
Go and Spread The good News!

1064. Gertrude Tabuwe Sirri Ngongba
That's awesome! Congratulations! This day can never be forgotten by some of us ooh.

1065. Pruddy Ghong
You deserve the love of all. You have a heart of gold. May God keep you strong and give you many beautiful years years to work in His vineyard. The world loves you

1066. Gladys Ajubese
Father it was lock mop ooh. We thank God for everything.

1067. Pamela Tegha
You deserve it father. God is going move you from glory to glory. You are a great man of God that transforms lives of individuals, families, Nations and the world at large. More blessings pardre.

1068. Caroline Tenye
What a great day

1069. Scholastic Awala
You deserve the love of all your mothers of the church. (CWA). CWO Mami them. You have a heart of gold. You are a good Shepherd. May God keep you strong well body. Bless and Protects Guide you throughout the days of your life. May He give you many more years in his ministry.

1070. Auntiefaus Nimongum
Congratulations Father.

1071. Gertrude Tabuwe Sirri Ngongba
That is awesome father, I was there.

1072. Maurice Akwa
Gertrude Tabuwe Sirri Ngongba I felt loved

1073. Chia Joan
Maurice Akwa you are loved

1074. Jane Bebs
Well-done ooooooh Pater.

1075. Immaculate Che
Congratulations.

1076. Magdalene Orock
Fr you are Honored and Blessed.

1077. Priscilla Neng Mulesiwi
Congratulations

1078. Chi Clement Mekolefagh
Great, Padre.

1079. Anna Ngu
Congratulations and thank God all went well.

1080. Emmanuel Moma Kisob
Congratulations and happy Feast Day. Mass today was fantastic.

1081. Jane Bebs
Happy feast of Christ the king Pater.

1082. Nfam Tosam Mukong
God bless you Father

1083. Priscilla Neng Mulesiwi
Jesus, I trust in you

1084. Chia Joan
Congratulations again father and happy feast of christ the king

1085. Naomi Blessings
God bless you more.

1086. Julius Ngole
My finest big bro.

1087. Assumpta Aba
Happy feast of Christ the King.

1088. Angelica Bih
This is the man. Our epic hero

1089. Niba-Ahlijah Meh Niba-Ahlijah
Nyuuiigong fahhh mboneehhh Tah father.

1090. Mimi La Belle Maurice Akwa

Congratulations fada! 25 good years in priestlyhood is not a joke. We praise and thank the most Holy God for your life Fr. Maurice Akwa. We thank you for your years of service and ask God to bless you, with many more years. Amen.

1091. Mbanga Rose

Happy Anniversary. The Most High has kept you strong in His vineyard to take care of His sheep. May He continue to bless you so that you carry His divine praises on earth

1092. Mbanga Rose

God is your strength

1093. Assumpta Bourgeois

Congratulations Fada! Continue to do what you love best.... serving God's people!

1094. Afanwi Lum

Oh wow!!! Congratulations Father. The good God has been faithful. We thank him for all the lives you have impacted over these years. You have no idea. Miyaka Yahweh. Thanks to you too Father Maurice for answering the call. Happy anniversary.

1095. Asonglefac Nkemleke
We raise a Hallelujah and say Thank You Lord. Continue to bless and keep Your Servant.

1096. Mimi La Belle
Congratulations Fada! This calls for celebrating. You are worthy to be celebrated.

1097. Eddy Etawo
Happy Anniversary Fr. Maurice. You have simply been an amazing spiritual inspiration to millions of Christians across the globe. May God continue to love. bless and guide you.

1098. Jean-françois Ebah
Joyeux anniversaire sacerdotal. Que Dieu achève en vous ce qu'il a si bien commencé

1099. Leonard Ngumbah
We shall be there to celebrate with you Father. Congratulations on your silver jubilee!!! More power to you for your workmanship in His vineyard

1100. Prodencia Asaba
Happy Anniversary father.

1101. Anne Francis
Congratulations Father, more wins in His Vineyard as you indefatigably spread the Word to the ends of the Earth. God continue to strengthen, protect and bless you throughout this journey.

1102. Therese Mezigue
Félicitations mon papa le temps passe vite

1103. Bruno Kuumtem
Happy anniversary fada I remember that wonderful day at St Martin parish Wum. May the Almighty Father continue to bless you and give you strength and wisdom in leading his flock

1104. Jevis Mai-Akwa
How time flies. Congratulation's padre.

1105. Gladys Obale
Congratulations Father. That's a long time. We thank God for taking you this far.

1106. Auntiefaus Nimongum
Congratulations to you Father, God bless you. a go Dance. Happy Anniversary.

1107. Doc Mafor
cCongratulations Fada

1108. Manso Arrey
Make I go buy my dancing shoes keepam.

1109. Taba Eseme
Oh, My Daddy, Happy Anniversary FROM CHEF TABA and Family. May God continue to Bless and Protect you.... IJN

1110. Norbert Kum
Happy Priestly Anniversary Father may God Almighty continue to guide and protect you.

1111. Gnintedem Hugette Temgoua
Ameeen congratulations Father we give God all the Glory and Praise.

1112. Lem Ndiangang

Oh, how time flies congrates my dear n may our God continue to shower blessings n good health on you, miss you.

1113. Clem Eto

Happy Birthday ooo my father my father.

1114. Electra Ngum

Wow congratulations father may God continue to be your strength.

1115. Francis Bama

I was there with you twenty-five years ago and you are just as dedicated today as of when you submitted to winning souls for God's kingdom.

1116. Elian Mambo

Praise God!!!

1117. Ngufor Delphine

Happy anniversary father.

1118. Eric Igwacho

Praise the Lord! Happy Anniversary Father.

1119. Hedrine Tamajong
Congratulations Fr. We thank God for his grace upon you.

1120. Hassan Augustine Turay
To God be the glory! Wishes of good, good health, God's blessings, knowledge and wisdom in your vocation.

1121. Frinwei Achu Njihy
Congratulations Father. May the Lord keep your spiritual flame burning as 25 years back.

1122. Priscilla Neng Mulesiwi
Waaaaooooo ! Congratulations and more grace Padre.

1123. Rose Rose
Joyeux anniversaire mon père que le seigneur te donne la force de continuer Son œuvre.

1124. Yega Elizabeth
Congratulations Father. The lord will continue to give you strength as you continue in this journey.

1125. Cloudatte Akwen

Wow, Congratulations Father. Wishing you many more fruitful years and celebration. The Lord is your strength.

1126. Damian Tem

I remember I handed over a gift on behalf of the school prefects and catholics of GHS Wum 1997/98 Batch. You tapped me on the back and said you once were a senior prefect of that very prestigious college and that i should stay focused. We will gladly.

1127. Nju Ghong Mercy Mbong

Congrats father.

1128. Julet Okafor

Congratulations and more grace father.

1129. Elizabeth Wachong

Congratulations, happy anniversary father, you will always be an inspirational force to many.

1130. Jinoh Jamet Banjong

More Strength Father! Wishing you all the best as you continue your divine journey of service in the vineyard of the Most high. CONGRATULATIONS !

1131. Héritier Polomayo

Je rends grâce à Dieu pour ces merveilles en votre faveur. Heureux jubilé d'argent mon Père.

1132. Francis Ebeke

Yes. Padre.

1133. Ethel Chu Buh

I was there; flower girl/cadet of Mary....can't forget that solemn procession. Glory be to God and a big congratulations to you Fr Mau. Date saved.

1134. Yvonne Tum

You've been up to the task for the work assigned to you 25 years ago. I pray for continuous favours upon your life and your duties. Congratulation's mon Padre.

1135. Niba-Ahlijah Meh Niba-Ahlijah

Congratulations Tah father.

1136. Bessong Arah

Congratulation Man of God.

1137. Abunaw Patience
Happy anniversary Father.

1138. Oliver Asaah
Happy anniversary Father.

1139. Taniform Taniform
Happy 25 anniversary.

1140. Kejetue Perpetua
Waoh waoh waoh. Happy silver jubilee. You are a priest forever like melchizede of old. Wishing you a blissful anniversary as you celebrate God's blessings in your life.its a fruitful mission. We continue to thank God for making you win more souls for Christ.

1141. Larrisa Azeteh
Congratulations Mon père. The journey has been Grace filled all along.

1142. Sih Enyowe
Congratulations my Fada. 25 years at God's service. May His name be praised.

1143. Pamela Mbuh
Wow happy anniversary ooooh.

1144. Nkongho Lucy Enoru
Happy anniversary Fada.

1145. Irine Ekanjume
Congratulations Fr.

1146. Nkwa Nih
More grace to your elbow.

1147. Julius Ngole
Happy Anniversary servant of God! Blessings.

1148. Brandino Kuwong
Congrats Father and happy anniversary.

1149. Loreta Yah
Hearty congratulations. Thanks for the services rendered to the people of God this far.

1150. Abraham Akih

What a milestone in ministry. We give thanks to God for 25years of dedicated service to the Lord God Almighty. Congratulations and more of his abiding grace in ministry.

1151. Wallang Ernest

I can imagine ur visits during pastoral formation at the holy ghost chapel in Btoua.

1152. Shey Limmy Dubila

Congratulations mon père. We shall be there.

1153. Fonge Vivian

Congratulations ooo Work Man for God. Many more gracefilled returns.

1154. Karin Awa

Congratulations and more blessings Father.

1155. Bernardine Audrey Yaya Wirnkar

How can we repay the Lord for the good he has done to us? To God be the glory. May he continue to be your strength.

1156. Banla Euginia
Congratulations and happy anniversary Father.

1157. Theresia Ngeniform
Congratulations.

1158. Vita Donvialli
25 years of feeding God's flock with spiritual food. Thanks for your service and we pray for for more energy and zeal to keep going...if I miss the 25th anniversary, I will certainly not miss the 50th.

1159. Kang Lucia
Happy Priestly Anniversary Father. Many more anniversaries to celebrate in God's vineyard.

1160. Wirsiy Yujika
Happy anniversary Fr. Many more ahead of you.

1161. Kum Edith Ewo
Congratulation's pater.

1162. Celest Tatung
God is faithful Le Pere. He will continue to bless and protect.

1163. Elizabeth Mbayu
Congratulations Fada. Abundant blessings.

1164. Mah Fidelia
Happy anniversary in advance Father and congratulations. May the Lord continue to bless, guide and protect you in His vineyard.

1165. Ngwen Niba
Congratulation's padre and may he continue to endow u with wisdom, patience, endurance and above all love and prayers.

1166. Olachi Joy Mezu-Ndubuisi
Congratulations Father Maurice. You are a priest forever. May God's love and blessings remain with you and continue to sustain your ministry. You are a blessing to us all.

1167. Ebonlo Grace
Congratulation's mon père thank u for feeding us with spiritual food may the good continue to shower u with his

blessings and strength to work in his Vin yard in the years a head.

1168. Assumpta Aba
Congratulations Father. More grace and blessings to you.

1169. Bertila Kongnyuy
Happy anniversary Father

1170. Therese Ngoin
Waoh! To God be the glory.

1171. Therese Ngoin
When is that?

1172. Roseta Ade
congratulations and many more years uploading

1173. Agnes Mbongere
Cool and congratulations Father.

1174. Patience Ndah
Congratulations Fr. Maurice. Many more years in the Lord's vineyard.

1175. George Nchumbonga-Chrysostom Lekelefac
Ad multos annos!

1176. Haoua Bobo
Happy Birthday padre...pluies de bénédictions au service du seigneur. Quil se souvienne de toi et t accorde les désirs de ton cœur.

1177. Taminang Pierre
Happy 25th anniversary of your priestly ordination in advance Rev. Father. May Almighty God bless you with many more years.

1178. Yvonne Fondufe-Mittendorf
Congratulations Fada. May God continue to bless you.

1179. Flore Mob
Oh, wow congratulations fada receive more blessings from your God Almighty.

1180. Rose Akwo
Happy 25th Priestley Anniversary my Fada.

1181. Bih Toyang
Congratulation's father. Many more years in the Lord's vineyard.

1182. Yaro Loveline Yula
Congratulations dear Father. May your work in His Vineyard be Blessed and be Blessings to us.

1183. Quinta Sangha
Congratulations Fada Mau may God continue to give u the wisdom and good health to serve His people. Thanks for all you do.

1184. Immaculate Che
Congratulations Papa.

1185. Grace Asaba
Yessss ooooh, he has made it, Satan is a liar. Many more fruitful years in God's fields. Happy 25th anniversary Padre.

1186. Mod Binam
J'attends ooo mon père.

1187. Rita Sondengam-Nyembe
Congratulations Fada!

1188. Divine Nchamukong
Congratulations Father Maurice.

1189. Bea Prisca
Wahoooooo A DIEU SEUL LA GLOIRE.

1190. Kiven Louis Ntahtin
I don mark the date.

1191. Neba Veritas Ngum
Congratulation's papa.

1192. Justina Ngeh
Congratulations Fada. Happy anniversary.

1193. Emmanuel Moma Kisob
Padre, Gratias agimus Deo.

1194. Joahana Mambo Tingem-Locker
Happy Anniversary Father.

1195. Bernadette Atanga
Happy Anniversary.

1196. Rosy Touh
CONGRATULATIONS FADA. THANK GOD FOR BRINGING YOU THIS FAR. WISHING YOU MANY MORE YEARS IN GOD'S VINEYARD. MAY HE CONTINUE TO PROTECT, GUIDE. BLESS AND GRANT YOU MORE WISDOM.

1197. Jane Bebs
Waoooo Pater. Congratulations and happy anniversary in advance.

1198. Mispa Nkematabong
Wow I can't wait.

1199. Zie Nji Atang
Congratulations Fada Maurice.

1200. Gladys Ajubese
Hehhh...Happy happy anniversary father.

1201. Terri Bueno
Happy and Blessed Anniversary.

1202. Vivian Acha-Morfaw
Yes, oh father huge congratulations.

1203. Magdalene Orock
Congratulations, Good Job in The Lord's Vineyard.

1204. Viban Helen
Congratulations Fada Maurice.

1205. Love Teumo
This is a great day to celebrate. God is good of can't wait to celebrate this great milestone with my favorite priest.

1206. Ndum Juliana
Congratulations my priest and happy anniversary.

1207. Love Teumo
Calendar marked.

1208. Mabel Nkembeng
Congratulations Father.

1209. Linda Akwa
Congratulations and happy anniversary, father. Blessings abound.

1210. Erika Indira Zara
Congrats Fada.

1211. Belinda Chungong
Congrats fada. Happy anniversary. May the Lord Continue to guide you as you work in His vineyard. Thanks for all you do.

1212. Pascal Tantoh
To God be the glory, Amen.

1213. Jemimah Chuks
Congratulation's sir.

1214. Christie Ngale
Happy priestly anniversary Father.

1215. Ojong Roseline Nkongho
Congratulations, my Rev. May God continue to give you more Grace and wisdom for you to continue to serve your people.

1216. Stella Fru
God is faithful. Congratulations on your 25th Anniversary Fada Maurice.

1217. Rita Cham
Happy blessed anniversary, my father, the best.

1218. Gus Bessong
Congratulations Fada!

1219. Mary Takwa
Congratulations Fad!!! May his light shine on you abundantly as you minister to his flock.

1220. Bimenyuy Viban
Padre congratulations.

1221. Maggi Akwa
Congratulations. Can't wait for the celebrations.

1222. Ngwa Angeline
Congratulation Fr. May the Lord continue to bless you with good health. Happy anniversary.

1223. Eunice Gwanmesia
Congratulations Father! May God continue to lead you!

1224. Anna Ngu
Amen oh Father. Can't wait to celebrate you and for thanking God for allowing you shepherd us for a quarter century. Miyaka.

1225. Millbrigg Simon Spencer
Great things the Lord worked for us. Celebrations awaiting.

1226. Evelyn Angu

Happy happy congratulations to you Fada. May your blessings continually higher and higher.

1227. Armstrong Ikoh Awani

Congratulations Father Happy Anniversary.

1228. Virginie Tashi

Happy anniversary Padre. May the Lord continue to bless you throughout this journey.

1229. Seh Gladys

Congratulations Fada.

1230. Philip Ngundam

To God be the Glory, my dear brother.

1231. Marc Ndifor

May be an image of text that says, 'God is the only reason I made it this far.'

1232. Paulette Synajie

Good morning padre.

1233. Kela Delphine Njike-Tah
Congratulations Fada. More Blessings.

1234. Mawo Regine
Wow congratulations in advance Father. Date noted.

1235. Endy Madukwe
Almighty God will continue to bless and protect you to continue your services to humanity.

1236. Njua Christina
Congratulation's father. May the Almighty God continue to bless you with good health. Stay lifted.

1237. Priscilla Woye
Congratulations Father.

1238. Rose Achoh
Congratulations Fr. Maurice. May the good Lord continue to give you the strength, health and wisdom to work in his vineyard. Wishing you many more blessings.

1239. Besongha Zembeh
Happy anniversary Father.

1240. Lucie Ngongbo
Congratulations Fada.

1241. Edward Cheng
Happy Silver jubilee in advance. It coincides with my birthday.

1242. Immaculate Chongwain Tedji
Congrats Father Maurice.

1243. Caroline Chita
Wow! Congrats Fada and happy anniversary.

1244. Mimi Ambe
Congratulations and best wishes on your 25th Anniversary of Priesthood Fr Mau. May God's goodness and kindness be with you on this special day and all the days of your life. God bless you and may He keep you safe in the palm of His hand.

1245. Ban John Beghabe Blaise
Congratulations to you Father for this Great Milestone. May the Good Lord continue to protect and guide you.

1246. Florence Ngundam
Amen!!! Congratulations.

1247. Esther
God bless you Rev. Father Maurice. Thank you for what you do for the Kingdom of God.

1248. Kamdem Njomo
Amazing. The Almighty is in action.

1249. McLyonga Liwoungwa Mota Wenama
Congratulations.

1250. Chi Gillian
Congratulations Padre. Happy anniversary in advance.

1251. Tanwani Esther
Amen.

1252. Nkwenti Grace Annette
Silver bells in the air! The date has been saved. Congratulations in advance Padre.

1253. Tangka Bongmah
HAPPY 25TH ANNIVERSARY FATHER!!!

1254. Evelyn Bridget
Congratulation's father happy anniversary in advance.

1255. Kpah Gregoryachuo
Happy anniversary my Lord.

1256. Ntaintain Nyiaseh
Congratulation's father.

1257. Gwen Tanyi
I will be there.

1258. Maurice Akwa
Gwen Tanyi my honor to have you.

1259. Nancy Bruns
such an honor, you are the best of the Greatest of our Holy Catholic Priests. Blessed Regards, Nancy Bruns.

1260. Clemantine Fonkeng
Congratulation's father.

1261. Mary Florence Chia
Congratulations Fr. Waiting anxiously for that day

1262. Chi Clement Mekolefagh
To God be the Glory. Happy Silver Jubilee Father. A True worker in the Vineyard.

1263. Mary Chilla
Our father Happy anniversary. Congratulations, celebration, congrats and party.

1264. Mbunwe Colette
Congratulations to you Fr many more years in the Lord's vineyard.

1265. Camilla Tamasang
Congratulations Father Maurice.

1266. Bessem Ojong
Happy anniversary in advance Fada Mau.

1267. Nkenyi Claris
Congrats Fada Maurice. The Lord is your strength. May he continue to guard your path.

1268. Attoh Moutchia
Congratulations Father. May the Holy Spirit continue to be with you.

1269. Eunice Neba Ekani
Bug Congrats Father Maurice.

1270. Wency Nkem
What a milestone. Congratulations Fada and waiting for the big day.

1271. Emelda Ngwe
Congrats Father Maurice. I wish you many more years.

1272. Kel MNnbu
Huge congrats dearest Father Maurice.

1273. Chris Fokumlah
Congratulations and Happy Anniversary

1274. Claudia Kouamen
Félicitations father. Que le seigneur continue de te guider.

1275. Nicolyne Fonjie Idem
Congratulations in arrears Padre

1276. Maurice Akwa
Nicolyne Fonjie Idem in advance sweetheart

1277. Rosimex Ndasi
Happy Happy oh Father. May the Good Lord increases in you His Wisdom to continue to lead His Sheep as you work in His Vineyard.

1278. Grace Ngum Awantu
Congratulations Rev. To God be the glory.

1279. Micheline Mich
Congratulation's father.

1280. Nange Mary May
Congratulations Padre.

1281. Beatrice Moma
Congratulations Fada Maurice Akwa.

1282. Roland Patcha
Mighty congratulations Padre Maurice! Thank you for your divine service and guidance!
God be with you!

1283. Glory Udom
Congratulations. I will be there.

1284. Maurice Akwa
Glory Udom joyfully joyfully, my joy!

1285. Marlyse Mbanga
Congratulation's mon père.

1286. Lukong Eunice
Thanks, so much, father for choosing the right path.

1287. Clarence Ndangam
Congrats Father Maurice. Dates marked and can't wait!

1288. Jim Fleming
I really want to be there. Please keep updates.

1289. Scholastic Awala
Continue to be the good Shepherd you are, The Man up there who sees even in darkness, will reward you million-fold. Amen.

1290. Julia Buban Ngu
Congratulations fr for this special gift from God.and happy anniversary. We are together you.

1291. Nenge Azefor Njongmeta
Congratulations on your Silver Jubilee Father. Wishing you more years in His vineyard.

1292. Colette Tamangwa
Happy anniversary Father.

1293. Sabina Jules
Congratulation's father. Wishing you good heath as you help us to grow in faith.

1294. Lucille Munchi
Congratulation's padre in advance!!!

1295. Lucille Munchi
I guess you will join me first on November 8!!!

1296. Assoua Emmanuel
I sayeee years are running! Happy Anniversary Father Maurice.

1297. Ernestine Besong
Happy anniversary Father.

1298. Lydia Ekeme
The work of the Almighty.

1299. Duchess K Lira
I was there! I will be there!

1300. Maurice Akwa
Duchess K Lira my eyewitness baby

1301. Duchess K Lira
Maurice Akwa yours always, Fada.

1302. Rose Vershiyi
Congratulations Father. Thank you so much for the beautiful work you've been doing to the people of God. You have been a wonderful Shepherd. May God, guide you continue the work in His vineyard

1303. Justine Fomekong Jou
Félicitations padre.

1304. Nkamsi Besong
Woah congrats ooooo Father. We thank God ooooh for taking you this far and pray God will bless you more and more.

1305. Rosemary Niba
Happy anniversary Father and congratulations.

1306. Asong Amingwa Jude
More wins in His vineyard.

1307. Therese Suiru Marie
Congratulations Father and happy anniversary.

1308. Oben Afah
Happy anniversary father.

1309. James Achuo
Congratulations Father and continue with the good work. God bless.

1400. Enow Christain
May the Good lord who has inspired you all this while continue to make a way for you father. The lord is your strength. Jesus l trust in You.

1401. Nji Rosaline
Happy anniversary, we pray for protection, good health and wisdom to continue the good work in God's vineyard.

1402. Mbianda Grace
Congratulations and many more 25 years to come fada.

1403. Zebedee T Yong
Happy anniversary Father Maurice Akwa.

1404. Gertrude Tabuwe Sirri Ngongba
Congrats and happy anniversary in advance father.

1405. Azinwi Fuh
Congratulations in advance Fada. May God continue to be your strength.

1406. Gladys Lantum Achiri
Congratulations Fada Mau.

1407. Lidwina Kroll
Wow, wow congratulations Padre. See how time flies. We thank God for taking you this far. More grace in God's vineyard.

1408. Joh Cecilia
Father Maurice, happy anniversary oooo. May the good work you started be brought to fulfiillment.

1409. Pamela Tegha
Congrats in advance father.

1410. Odilia Mambo Akuma
Waoh, happy anniversary Father and many more graceful years ahead.

1411. Cloudatte Akwen
Happy Anniversary Father.

1412. Clotilde Ngante
Great. We thank God for the gift of priesthood Father Maurice.

1413. Laura Ngwana
Congratulations......Bless you.

1414. Pruddy Ghong
Wowwww congratulations ohhhh. You are so blessed. I have marked the date ohhhhh.

1415. Florence Uche
Congratulations Fr more blessings from God

1416. Catherine Atesiri Ambe
Happy Aniversary my reverend. I wish you many more years.

1417. Catherine Atesiri Ambe
And more more wisdom and be cover by the precious blood of Jesus.

1418. Nfon Maurine
Congratulations, Pedre.

1419. Ebony Shudelphine
Congrats Padre.

1420. Jessica Kini
Congratulations Fr. I'll be there.

1421. Mirabel Tandafor
Congratulations Father.

1422. Juskall Meedocktorr
Congratulations Fr. May God continue to bless your priestly journey.

1423. Charles Osong
Proud of you, Fada. You are a true servant of the most high. I pray to be around so I can witness the bitter/sweet event live.

1424. Martha F. Langdon
Congratulations! I'll be praying for you!!!

1425. Jesse Chi
Congratulation padre.

1426. Adel Etia
Congratulations Complice. Many more anniversaries is my wish for you.

1427. Dorothy Mensah-Aggrey
Glory to God.

1428. Caroline Yancy-Anih
Congratulations Father!

1429. Odilia Fri Mundi Wankwi
We thank God for taking you this far into your Priestly Ministry. To God be all the Glory. Congratulations Padre.

1430. Martina Mofoke

Congratulations Padre. It has been an awesome journey as many souls have been drawn to the Lord. May God continue to strengthen you and bless you abundantly.

1431. Betty Etonde

Happy anniversary Father. May God continue to bless you as you work in His vineyard.

1432. Rachel Ojong

Congratulations Fada.

1433. Elodie A. Tendoh

Yes, ohhh father, can't wait to celebrate with you. Congratulations in advance.

1434. Theresia Fuh-Tabe

Well done! the good Lord will continue to uphold you with His right hand. More grace Reverend.

1435. Tim Finnian

Congratulations Fala.

1436. Anthony Mboh
Congratulations fada.

1437. Gwendoline Atabong Nkumbah
Wow father, time flies. God is faithful, thank God you kept your faith and his goodness in your life is shown all over you. Praying this great day comes to reality. Celebration uploading.

1438. Debora Fon-aleh Wilson
Congratulations father Mau. God's blessings oooo.

1439. Galega Kenneth
Congratulations Fr Maurice.

1440. Geraldine Tumenta
Congratulations. Muchas Felicidades, felicidades, BIENHECHO, FIESTA.

1441. Geraldine Tumenta
Congratulations on your 25th year of Priesthood. You plain rock Father. Keep soaring to new heights and praying for us sinners to repent. More years to your belt. Stay blessed with the Lord. Always Manyi Mom and Grandma.

1442. Jacqueline Mukala Wainfein
Congratulations Father.

1443. Hycentha Lai
Congratulations Father Maurice.

1444. Eveline Ncho
Congratulations.

1445. Bih Virgilia
Congratulations Father Akwa. The Lord is your strength.

1446. Moki Charles Linonge
Happy anniversary Fada Maurice Akwa. We have saved the date.

1447. Nibalum Elizabeth
Happy anniversary fada.

1448. Lucien Enguele Ebogo
Happy anniversary. Congratulation's father.

1449. Jane Mobufor

Congratulations my dear father Mau. God's blessings are always on you.

1450. Brunhilda Asamba

Happy anniversary in advance father.

1451. Rose Mary Suh

Happy silver jubilee patre in advance. May the Good Lord continue to increase in you and may you decrease for his glory in the name of Jesus name.

1452. Rose Mary Suh

Happy Anniversary Father Maurice.

1453. Rose Mezu

Happy ordination Anniversary, Fr. Maurice Akwa, a priest in the Order of Melchizedek! And, of course, it has to fall on my Birthday!!'

1454. Rose Mezu

Bon anniversaire!!!

1455. Bonaventure Ngu
Congrats Father Maurice.

1456. Gabriel Asaba
Congrats Father.

1457. Robert Sears
Congratulations Fr Maurice.

1458. Solange Lomessoas
Joyeux jubilé d'argent.

1459. Lionel Ayuk
Congratulations Father Maurice.

1460. Ngwen Niba
I can never thank God enough for the gift of impacting the lifes of others especially me. May God Continue to bless, protect, guard and guide, as you keep working for the good of the church.

1461. Cinta Ngu
Happy anniversary Mon Pere! Lots of love and prayers for you always.

1462. Winifred Leogaa Fofuleng
Congratulations in advance. Can't wait.

1463. Frankaline Ley
Happy anniversary Father Maurice.

Chapter Three: An encomium to Reverend Father Maurice Akwa, by Nchumbonga George Lekelefac

An encomium to Reverend Father Maurice Akwa [Bachelor's in Philosophy, Pontificia Universitas Urbaniana, Rome (1990); Bachelors in Theology, Catholic University for Central Africa Yaoundé (1996); STL in Sacred Theology specializing in Sacred Scripture, St. Mary's Seminary and University Baltimore, USA (2007); Doctorate Fellow in Pastoral Clinical Psycho-Therapy]; illustrious Diocesan Spiritual Director for Catholic Men and Catholic Women's Associations; exemplary Cameroonian ambassador and missionary in the USA; erudite Diocesan Ecumenical Coordinator; well-known Chaplain and Coordinator of the Association of Widows and Orphans; legendary scripture scholar and lecturer; expert in

Reverend Father Doctorandus Maurice Akwa: 25th Priestly Anniversary Festschrift (15.11.1997 - 15.11.2022), Volume 1. Edited by Nchumbonga George Lekelefac

Pastoral Clinical Psycho-Therapy; talented and gifted musician and singer; celebrated basketball coached; eminent choir conductor; one of the founding fathers of the Cameroon Catholic Community for the Washington DC Metro area (March 2006); highly distinguished dramatist; outstanding playwright; pastor with the smell of the sheep with an outstanding passion for the sick, underprivileged and the aging; on the occasion of his 58th birthday celebration [September 22, 1963 – September 22, 2021], written by Nchumbonga George Lekelefac, Doctorate Candidate, Westfälische Wilhelms-Universität, Münster, Germany, Wednesday, September 22, 2021

Introduction

This encomium is dedicated to Reverend Father Maurice Akwa on the occasion of his 58th birthday celebration. May the name of the Lord be praised both now and forever. Amen. The Lord is good, all the time, and all the time, the Lord is good.

Fr. Maurice Akwa was born in Weh, Northwest Region of Cameroon, but ordained priest for the Archdiocese of Bertoua in the East Region of Cameroon. He has a first degree in Philosophy and in Theology, as well as a Licentiate in Sacred Theology specializing in Biblical Theology which he taught for 15 years in the Major Seminary in Bertoua. He has been a priest for 23 years and is now on a temporal academic residence in Maryland, completing an online doctorate in Pastoral Clinical Psychotherapy. Fr. Akwa is a Roman Catholic Diocesan priest from Cameroon. He has served as director of schools in three dioceses combined for three years and being a formator in the Major Seminary for 14 years, which has made his world view very broad and humbling. His mindset knows no borders. As a pastor of souls, he has come to realize how fragile we are as humans and remain open 24/7 to be online and direct assistance to all. He is presently in Residence at St. Charles Borromeo Church in Pikesville, MD, Archdiocese of Baltimore, USA

My encounters with Father Akwa Maurice

I got to know about Father Akwa Maurice on social media. What attracted me to his Facebook page were his unfaltering Sunday reflections on Facebook. Thus, we became friends so many years ago on Facebook and I looked forward to meeting him in person someday.

Fortunately, I betook myself from Dallas, Texas on September 4 to Baltimore to attend the first mass of the first Cameroonian-born Bishop in the United States of America: Bishop Jerome Feudjio. During that occasion, I was graced to meet and encounter Father Akwa Maurice for the very first time in my life. It was a very graceful and joyful meeting. He easily recognized me when I approached him after mass, and I was surprised when he exclaimed: "That you for all the work and interest you are doing for the Church.". Later, I presented to him my 1085-page research book on Professor Doctor Bernard Nsokika Fonlon. He was excited and we spoke briefly due to the fact that a long line of Christian faithful was waiting to greet him too. He is highly approachable and very friendly priest who devotes time for the Christian faithful despite his extremely busy schedule. In summary, my meeting and encounter with Father Maurice Akwa at St Camillus Parish, at Maryland was highly remarkable and unforgettable. Thank you, father, for being so nice and for inspiring me to profound my knowledge in scripture. Let us now have an idea of who Father Maurice is.

Brief Biography

Father Maurice Akwa was Born in Small Soppo on September 22, 1963, Fr. Maurice Akwa decided to become a priest on the feast of St Stephen, 26th December 1971, shortly after his 1st Holy Communion. He has been to Minor seminary, 1978-1983, worked in Sonel Wum, 1983-85, and attended Government High School Wum 1985-87 before going to Bambui 1987. It is when he was not allowed to return to Bambui after his pastoral year in Small Mankon 1990-1991, during the hot days of SDF that he taught in Sacred Heart College Mankon 1991-1993 before joining the Archdiocese of Bertoua and sent to do Theology in the Catholic University Yaoundé.

Academic qualifications

He holds a Bachelor's in Philosophy from St. Thomas Aquinas Major Seminary in Bambui Cameroon (1990), bachelor's in theology from the Catholic University for Central Africa Yaounde (1996), and STL in Theology specializing in Sacred Scripture from St. Mary's Seminary and University Baltimore (2007). [SLT: Sacrae Theologiae Licentiatus, which translates as "licentiate of sacred theology"] from 2004 – 2007.

Presently, he is on a temporal academic residence in Maryland, completing an online doctorate in Pastoral Clinical Psychotherapy.

Pastoral assignments

Reverend Father Doctorandus Maurice Akwa: 25th Priestly Anniversary Festschrift (15.11.1997 - 15.11.2022), Volume 1. Edited by Nchumbonga George Lekelefac

Father Maurice Akwa has served as: 1) Secretary for Catholic education for the Ecclesiastical province of Bertoua Cameroon (four dioceses) (1996-1999); 2) Lecturer in the major seminary (1998-2004, 2007-2015); 3) Spiritual director of the seminary (1999-2000); 4) Rector of the Spiritual year (2000-2002); 5) Assistant parish priest (1999-2002); 6) Parish priest (2002-2004).

Fr Maurice Akwa: Diocesan Spiritual Director for Catholic Men and Catholic Women's Associations

Among other things, he has been Diocesan Spiritual Director for Catholic Men and Catholic Women's Associations, Diocesan Ecumenical Coordinator as well as leading Chaplain and Coordinator of the Association of Widows and Orphans.

Fr Maurice Akwa: Scripture scholar

He has been a scripture scholar since June 2007 – present, a period of about 14 years 4 months). His Sunday reflections on Facebook reflect the expertise that he has for scripture.

Fr Maurice Akwa: man of languages – polyglot

Father Maurice speaks English, French. He is perfectly bilingual. In addition, he also has knowledge on Italian, Spanish and some German. He has a good knowledge of Hebrew and Greek.

Fr Maurice Akwa: man of music

Fr. Maurice Akwa loved Music all his life, being member of school choirs from primary school to higher education and choir conductor for 18 years.

Fr Maurice Akwa: Basketball coach

Fr. Maurice Akwa coached basketball for two years and was Student University President in the Catholic University Yaoundé 1995/96.

Fr Maurice Akwa: dramatist and playwright

Fr. Maurice Akwa acted drama with the seminary troop and a public theatre club, the Merry Troopers, with Ayah Paul.

Fr Maurice Akwa: founding member of the Cameroon Catholic Community for the Washington DC.

As a student at St Mary's seminary in Baltimore 2004-2007, with other ex-seminarians from Bambui in association with close friends, they, including Fr. Maurice Akwa nursed the idea of the creation of a Cameroon Catholic Community for the Washington DC Metro area and this was hatched in March 2006. Since then, the Cameroonians have a wonderful catholic community in Washington.

Fr Maurice Akwa: passionate for the sick, underprivileged and the aging

Fr. Maurice Akwa is passionate for the sick,

underprivileged and the aging. He is a true and genuine pastor who cares for the sheep entrusted to him and those far away.

Fr Maurice Akwa: great homilist and preacher

Fr Maurice is sound in scripture and an exceptional homilist. If you listen to his homilies online, you will be inspired by his soundness of doctrine and teachings. In addition, he is an exceptional speaker who can hold the assembly spellbound for so many hours without then getting bored.

Conclusion

Rev Fr Maurice Akwa: Happy birthday! Wishing you many more years of longlife, good health, constant joy and happiness, and the realisation of all your dreams and projects. Dear Be rest assured of my prayers for you as you continue to serve as a devoted priest and educationist in the vineyard of God. Keep on taking the good initiatives and doing the good work. May you be blessed both now and forever. Amen.

Happy Birthday! (English); Alles Gute zum Geburtstag! (German); Buon compleanno! (italiano); Joyeux anniversaire! (French); ¡Feliz cumpleaños! (Spanish); Feliz aniversário! (Portuguese); gelukkige verjaardag (Dutch). Best wishes!

This encomium was respectfully, devotedly, affectionately, and prayerfully submitted for publication, today, Wednesday, September 23, 2021.

This Encomium was written by Nchumbonga George Lekelefac, B. Phil. (Mexico), STB. (Roma), JCL/MCL.

(Ottawa); Diploma in English, French, Spanish, Italian, Portuguese, German, and Dutch; [Degrees earned in order to serve mankind better and not otherwise]; Doctorate Candidate at the Westfälische Wilhelms-Universität, Katholisch Theologische Fakultät, Ökumenisches Institut, Münster, Deutschland, Europe

Chapter Four: Pictures of Silver Jubilee Celebration of Fr Maurice Akwa

Reverend Father Doctorandus Maurice Akwa: 25th Priestly Anniversary Festschrift (15.11.1997 - 15.11.2022), Volume 1. Edited by Nchumbonga George Lekelefac

Reverend Father Doctorandus Maurice Akwa: 25th Priestly Anniversary Festschrift (15.11.1997 - 15.11.2022), Volume 1. Edited by Nchumbonga George Lekelefac

Reverend Father Doctorandus Maurice Akwa: 25th Priestly Anniversary Festschrift (15.11.1997 - 15.11.2022), Volume 1. Edited by Nchumbonga George Lekelefac

Reverend Father Doctorandus Maurice Akwa: 25th Priestly Anniversary Festschrift (15.11.1997 - 15.11.2022), Volume 1. Edited by Nchumbonga George Lekelefac

Reverend Father Doctorandus Maurice Akwa: 25th Priestly Anniversary Festschrift (15.11.1997 - 15.11.2022), Volume 1. Edited by Nchumbonga George Lekelefac

Reverend Father Doctorandus Maurice Akwa: 25th Priestly Anniversary Festschrift (15.11.1997 - 15.11.2022), Volume 1. Edited by Nchumbonga George Lekelefac

Reverend Father Doctorandus Maurice Akwa: 25th Priestly Anniversary Festschrift (15.11.1997 - 15.11.2022), Volume 1. Edited by Nchumbonga George Lekelefac

Reverend Father Doctorandus Maurice Akwa: 25th Priestly Anniversary Festschrift (15.11.1997 - 15.11.2022), Volume 1. Edited by Nchumbonga George Lekelefac

Reverend Father Doctorandus Maurice Akwa: 25th Priestly Anniversary Festschrift (15.11.1997 - 15.11.2022), Volume 1. Edited by Nchumbonga George Lekelefac

Reverend Father Doctorandus Maurice Akwa: 25th Priestly Anniversary Festschrift (15.11.1997 - 15.11.2022), Volume 1. Edited by Nchumbonga George Lekelefac

Reverend Father Doctorandus Maurice Akwa: 25th Priestly Anniversary Festschrift (15.11.1997 - 15.11.2022), Volume 1. Edited by Nchumbonga George Lekelefac

Reverend Father Doctorandus Maurice Akwa: 25th Priestly Anniversary Festschrift (15.11.1997 - 15.11.2022), Volume 1. Edited by Nchumbonga George Lekelefac

Reverend Father Doctorandus Maurice Akwa: 25th Priestly Anniversary Festschrift (15.11.1997 - 15.11.2022), Volume 1. Edited by Nchumbonga George Lekelefac

Reverend Father Doctorandus Maurice Akwa: 25th Priestly Anniversary Festschrift (15.11.1997 - 15.11.2022), Volume 1. Edited by Nchumbonga George Lekelefac

Reverend Father Doctorandus Maurice Akwa: 25th Priestly Anniversary Festschrift (15.11.1997 - 15.11.2022), Volume 1. Edited by Nchumbonga George Lekelefac

Reverend Father Doctorandus Maurice Akwa: 25th Priestly Anniversary Festschrift (15.11.1997 - 15.11.2022), Volume 1. Edited by Nchumbonga George Lekelefac

Reverend Father Doctorandus Maurice Akwa: 25th Priestly Anniversary Festschrift (15.11.1997 - 15.11.2022), Volume 1. Edited by Nchumbonga George Lekelefac

Reverend Father Doctorandus Maurice Akwa: 25th Priestly Anniversary Festschrift (15.11.1997 - 15.11.2022), Volume 1. Edited by Nchumbonga George Lekelefac

Reverend Father Doctorandus Maurice Akwa: 25th Priestly Anniversary Festschrift (15.11.1997 - 15.11.2022), Volume 1. Edited by Nchumbonga George Lekelefac

Reverend Father Doctorandus Maurice Akwa: 25th Priestly Anniversary Festschrift (15.11.1997 - 15.11.2022), Volume 1. Edited by Nchumbonga George Lekelefac

Reverend Father Doctorandus Maurice Akwa: 25th Priestly Anniversary Festschrift (15.11.1997 - 15.11.2022), Volume 1. Edited by Nchumbonga George Lekelefac

Reverend Father Doctorandus Maurice Akwa: 25th Priestly Anniversary Festschrift (15.11.1997 - 15.11.2022), Volume 1. Edited by Nchumbonga George Lekelefac

Reverend Father Doctorandus Maurice Akwa: 25th Priestly Anniversary Festschrift (15.11.1997 - 15.11.2022), Volume 1. Edited by Nchumbonga George Lekelefac

Reverend Father Doctorandus Maurice Akwa: 25th Priestly Anniversary Festschrift (15.11.1997 - 15.11.2022), Volume 1. Edited by Nchumbonga George Lekelefac

Reverend Father Doctorandus Maurice Akwa: 25th Priestly Anniversary Festschrift (15.11.1997 - 15.11.2022), Volume 1. Edited by Nchumbonga George Lekelefac

Reverend Father Doctorandus Maurice Akwa: 25th Priestly Anniversary Festschrift (15.11.1997 - 15.11.2022), Volume 1. Edited by Nchumbonga George Lekelefac

Reverend Father Doctorandus Maurice Akwa: 25th Priestly Anniversary Festschrift (15.11.1997 - 15.11.2022), Volume 1. Edited by Nchumbonga George Lekelefac

Reverend Father Doctorandus Maurice Akwa: 25th Priestly Anniversary Festschrift (15.11.1997 - 15.11.2022), Volume 1. Edited by Nchumbonga George Lekelefac

Reverend Father Doctorandus Maurice Akwa: 25th Priestly Anniversary Festschrift (15.11.1997 - 15.11.2022), Volume 1. Edited by Nchumbonga George Lekelefac

Reverend Father Doctorandus Maurice Akwa: 25th Priestly Anniversary Festschrift (15.11.1997 - 15.11.2022), Volume 1. Edited by Nchumbonga George Lekelefac

Reverend Father Doctorandus Maurice Akwa: 25th Priestly Anniversary Festschrift (15.11.1997 - 15.11.2022), Volume 1. Edited by Nchumbonga George Lekelefac

Reverend Father Doctorandus Maurice Akwa: 25th Priestly Anniversary Festschrift (15.11.1997 - 15.11.2022), Volume 1. Edited by Nchumbonga George Lekelefac

Reverend Father Doctorandus Maurice Akwa: 25th Priestly Anniversary Festschrift (15.11.1997 - 15.11.2022), Volume 1. Edited by Nchumbonga George Lekelefac

Reverend Father Doctorandus Maurice Akwa: 25th Priestly Anniversary Festschrift (15.11.1997 - 15.11.2022), Volume 1. Edited by Nchumbonga George Lekelefac

Reverend Father Doctorandus Maurice Akwa: 25th Priestly Anniversary Festschrift (15.11.1997 - 15.11.2022), Volume 1. Edited by Nchumbonga George Lekelefac

Reverend Father Doctorandus Maurice Akwa: 25th Priestly Anniversary Festschrift (15.11.1997 - 15.11.2022), Volume 1. Edited by Nchumbonga George Lekelefac

Reverend Father Doctorandus Maurice Akwa: 25th Priestly Anniversary Festschrift (15.11.1997 - 15.11.2022), Volume 1. Edited by Nchumbonga George Lekelefac

Reverend Father Doctorandus Maurice Akwa: 25th Priestly Anniversary Festschrift (15.11.1997 - 15.11.2022), Volume 1. Edited by Nchumbonga George Lekelefac

Reverend Father Doctorandus Maurice Akwa: 25th Priestly Anniversary Festschrift (15.11.1997 - 15.11.2022), Volume 1. Edited by Nchumbonga George Lekelefac

Reverend Father Doctorandus Maurice Akwa: 25th Priestly Anniversary Festschrift (15.11.1997 - 15.11.2022), Volume 1. Edited by Nchumbonga George Lekelefac

Reverend Father Doctorandus Maurice Akwa: 25th Priestly Anniversary Festschrift (15.11.1997 - 15.11.2022), Volume 1. Edited by Nchumbonga George Lekelefac

Reverend Father Doctorandus Maurice Akwa: 25th Priestly Anniversary Festschrift (15.11.1997 - 15.11.2022), Volume 1. Edited by Nchumbonga George Lekelefac

Reverend Father Doctorandus Maurice Akwa: 25th Priestly Anniversary Festschrift
(15.11.1997 - 15.11.2022), Volume 1. Edited by Nchumbonga George Lekelefac

Reverend Father Doctorandus Maurice Akwa: 25th Priestly Anniversary Festschrift (15.11.1997 - 15.11.2022), Volume 1. Edited by Nchumbonga George Lekelefac

Reverend Father Doctorandus Maurice Akwa: 25th Priestly Anniversary Festschrift (15.11.1997 - 15.11.2022), Volume 1. Edited by Nchumbonga George Lekelefac

Reverend Father Doctorandus Maurice Akwa: 25th Priestly Anniversary Festschrift (15.11.1997 - 15.11.2022), Volume 1. Edited by Nchumbonga George Lekelefac

Reverend Father Doctorandus Maurice Akwa: 25th Priestly Anniversary Festschrift (15.11.1997 - 15.11.2022), Volume 1. Edited by Nchumbonga George Lekelefac

Reverend Father Doctorandus Maurice Akwa: 25th Priestly Anniversary Festschrift (15.11.1997 - 15.11.2022), Volume 1. Edited by Nchumbonga George Lekelefac

Reverend Father Doctorandus Maurice Akwa: 25th Priestly Anniversary Festschrift (15.11.1997 - 15.11.2022), Volume 1. Edited by Nchumbonga George Lekelefac

Reverend Father Doctorandus Maurice Akwa: 25th Priestly Anniversary Festschrift (15.11.1997 - 15.11.2022), Volume 1. Edited by Nchumbonga George Lekelefac

Reverend Father Doctorandus Maurice Akwa: 25th Priestly Anniversary Festschrift
(15.11.1997 - 15.11.2022), Volume 1. Edited by Nchumbonga George Lekelefac

Reverend Father Doctorandus Maurice Akwa: 25th Priestly Anniversary Festschrift (15.11.1997 - 15.11.2022), Volume 1. Edited by Nchumbonga George Lekelefac

Reverend Father Doctorandus Maurice Akwa: 25th Priestly Anniversary Festschrift (15.11.1997 - 15.11.2022), Volume 1. Edited by Nchumbonga George Lekelefac

Reverend Father Doctorandus Maurice Akwa: 25th Priestly Anniversary Festschrift (15.11.1997 - 15.11.2022), Volume 1. Edited by Nchumbonga George Lekelefac

Reverend Father Doctorandus Maurice Akwa: 25th Priestly Anniversary Festschrift (15.11.1997 - 15.11.2022), Volume 1. Edited by Nchumbonga George Lekelefac

Reverend Father Doctorandus Maurice Akwa: 25th Priestly Anniversary Festschrift (15.11.1997 - 15.11.2022), Volume 1. Edited by Nchumbonga George Lekelefac

Reverend Father Doctorandus Maurice Akwa: 25th Priestly Anniversary Festschrift (15.11.1997 - 15.11.2022), Volume 1. Edited by Nchumbonga George Lekelefac

Reverend Father Doctorandus Maurice Akwa: 25th Priestly Anniversary Festschrift (15.11.1997 - 15.11.2022), Volume 1. Edited by Nchumbonga George Lekelefac

Reverend Father Doctorandus Maurice Akwa: 25th Priestly Anniversary Festschrift (15.11.1997 - 15.11.2022), Volume 1. Edited by Nchumbonga George Lekelefac

Reverend Father Doctorandus Maurice Akwa: 25th Priestly Anniversary Festschrift (15.11.1997 - 15.11.2022), Volume 1. Edited by Nchumbonga George Lekelefac

Reverend Father Doctorandus Maurice Akwa: 25th Priestly Anniversary Festschrift (15.11.1997 - 15.11.2022), Volume 1. Edited by Nchumbonga George Lekelefac

Reverend Father Doctorandus Maurice Akwa: 25th Priestly Anniversary Festschrift (15.11.1997 - 15.11.2022), Volume 1. Edited by Nchumbonga George Lekelefac

Reverend Father Doctorandus Maurice Akwa: 25th Priestly Anniversary Festschrift (15.11.1997 - 15.11.2022), Volume 1. Edited by Nchumbonga George Lekelefac

Reverend Father Doctorandus Maurice Akwa: 25th Priestly Anniversary Festschrift (15.11.1997 - 15.11.2022), Volume 1. Edited by Nchumbonga George Lekelefac

Reverend Father Doctorandus Maurice Akwa: 25th Priestly Anniversary Festschrift (15.11.1997 - 15.11.2022), Volume 1. Edited by Nchumbonga George Lekelefac

Reverend Father Doctorandus Maurice Akwa: 25th Priestly Anniversary Festschrift (15.11.1997 - 15.11.2022), Volume 1. Edited by Nchumbonga George Lekelefac

Reverend Father Doctorandus Maurice Akwa: 25th Priestly Anniversary Festschrift (15.11.1997 - 15.11.2022), Volume 1. Edited by Nchumbonga George Lekelefac

Reverend Father Doctorandus Maurice Akwa: 25th Priestly Anniversary Festschrift
(15.11.1997 - 15.11.2022), Volume 1. Edited by Nchumbonga George Lekelefac

Reverend Father Doctorandus Maurice Akwa: 25th Priestly Anniversary Festschrift (15.11.1997 - 15.11.2022), Volume 1. Edited by Nchumbonga George Lekelefac

Reverend Father Doctorandus Maurice Akwa: 25th Priestly Anniversary Festschrift (15.11.1997 - 15.11.2022), Volume 1. Edited by Nchumbonga George Lekelefac

Reverend Father Doctorandus Maurice Akwa: 25th Priestly Anniversary Festschrift (15.11.1997 - 15.11.2022), Volume 1. Edited by Nchumbonga George Lekelefac

Reverend Father Doctorandus Maurice Akwa: 25th Priestly Anniversary Festschrift (15.11.1997 - 15.11.2022), Volume 1. Edited by Nchumbonga George Lekelefac

Reverend Father Doctorandus Maurice Akwa: 25th Priestly Anniversary Festschrift (15.11.1997 - 15.11.2022), Volume 1. Edited by Nchumbonga George Lekelefac

Reverend Father Doctorandus Maurice Akwa: 25th Priestly Anniversary Festschrift
(15.11.1997 - 15.11.2022), Volume 1. Edited by Nchumbonga George Lekelefac

Reverend Father Doctorandus Maurice Akwa: 25th Priestly Anniversary Festschrift (15.11.1997 - 15.11.2022), Volume 1. Edited by Nchumbonga George Lekelefac

Reverend Father Doctorandus Maurice Akwa: 25th Priestly Anniversary Festschrift (15.11.1997 - 15.11.2022), Volume 1. Edited by Nchumbonga George Lekelefac

Reverend Father Doctorandus Maurice Akwa: 25th Priestly Anniversary Festschrift (15.11.1997 - 15.11.2022), Volume 1. Edited by Nchumbonga George Lekelefac

Reverend Father Doctorandus Maurice Akwa: 25th Priestly Anniversary Festschrift (15.11.1997 - 15.11.2022), Volume 1. Edited by Nchumbonga George Lekelefac

Reverend Father Doctorandus Maurice Akwa: 25th Priestly Anniversary Festschrift (15.11.1997 - 15.11.2022), Volume 1. Edited by Nchumbonga George Lekelefac

Reverend Father Doctorandus Maurice Akwa: 25th Priestly Anniversary Festschrift (15.11.1997 - 15.11.2022), Volume 1. Edited by Nchumbonga George Lekelefac

Reverend Father Doctorandus Maurice Akwa: 25th Priestly Anniversary Festschrift (15.11.1997 - 15.11.2022), Volume 1. Edited by Nchumbonga George Lekelefac

Reverend Father Doctorandus Maurice Akwa: 25th Priestly Anniversary Festschrift (15.11.1997 - 15.11.2022), Volume 1. Edited by Nchumbonga George Lekelefac

Reverend Father Doctorandus Maurice Akwa: 25th Priestly Anniversary Festschrift (15.11.1997 - 15.11.2022), Volume 1. Edited by Nchumbonga George Lekelefac

Reverend Father Doctorandus Maurice Akwa: 25th Priestly Anniversary Festschrift (15.11.1997 - 15.11.2022), Volume 1. Edited by Nchumbonga George Lekelefac

Reverend Father Doctorandus Maurice Akwa: 25th Priestly Anniversary Festschrift (15.11.1997 - 15.11.2022), Volume 1. Edited by Nchumbonga George Lekelefac

Reverend Father Doctorandus Maurice Akwa: 25th Priestly Anniversary Festschrift
(15.11.1997 - 15.11.2022), Volume 1. Edited by Nchumbonga George Lekelefac

Reverend Father Doctorandus Maurice Akwa: 25th Priestly Anniversary Festschrift (15.11.1997 - 15.11.2022), Volume 1. Edited by Nchumbonga George Lekelefac

Reverend Father Doctorandus Maurice Akwa: 25th Priestly Anniversary Festschrift (15.11.1997 - 15.11.2022), Volume 1. Edited by Nchumbonga George Lekelefac

Reverend Father Doctorandus Maurice Akwa: 25th Priestly Anniversary Festschrift (15.11.1997 - 15.11.2022), Volume 1. Edited by Nchumbonga George Lekelefac

Reverend Father Doctorandus Maurice Akwa: 25th Priestly Anniversary Festschrift
(15.11.1997 - 15.11.2022), Volume 1. Edited by Nchumbonga George Lekelefac

Reverend Father Doctorandus Maurice Akwa: 25th Priestly Anniversary Festschrift (15.11.1997 - 15.11.2022), Volume 1. Edited by Nchumbonga George Lekelefac

Reverend Father Doctorandus Maurice Akwa: 25th Priestly Anniversary Festschrift (15.11.1997 - 15.11.2022), Volume 1. Edited by Nchumbonga George Lekelefac

Reverend Father Doctorandus Maurice Akwa: 25th Priestly Anniversary Festschrift (15.11.1997 - 15.11.2022), Volume 1. Edited by Nchumbonga George Lekelefac

Reverend Father Doctorandus Maurice Akwa: 25th Priestly Anniversary Festschrift (15.11.1997 - 15.11.2022), Volume 1. Edited by Nchumbonga George Lekelefac

Reverend Father Doctorandus Maurice Akwa: 25th Priestly Anniversary Festschrift (15.11.1997 - 15.11.2022), Volume 1. Edited by Nchumbonga George Lekelefac

Reverend Father Doctorandus Maurice Akwa: 25th Priestly Anniversary Festschrift (15.11.1997 - 15.11.2022), Volume 1. Edited by Nchumbonga George Lekelefac

Reverend Father Doctorandus Maurice Akwa: 25th Priestly Anniversary Festschrift (15.11.1997 - 15.11.2022), Volume 1. Edited by Nchumbonga George Lekelefac

Reverend Father Doctorandus Maurice Akwa: 25th Priestly Anniversary Festschrift (15.11.1997 - 15.11.2022), Volume 1. Edited by Nchumbonga George Lekelefac

Reverend Father Doctorandus Maurice Akwa: 25th Priestly Anniversary Festschrift (15.11.1997 - 15.11.2022), Volume 1. Edited by Nchumbonga George Lekelefac

Reverend Father Doctorandus Maurice Akwa: 25th Priestly Anniversary Festschrift (15.11.1997 - 15.11.2022), Volume 1. Edited by Nchumbonga George Lekelefac

Reverend Father Doctorandus Maurice Akwa: 25th Priestly Anniversary Festschrift (15.11.1997 - 15.11.2022), Volume 1. Edited by Nchumbonga George Lekelefac

Reverend Father Doctorandus Maurice Akwa: 25th Priestly Anniversary Festschrift (15.11.1997 - 15.11.2022), Volume 1. Edited by Nchumbonga George Lekelefac

Reverend Father Doctorandus Maurice Akwa: 25th Priestly Anniversary Festschrift (15.11.1997 - 15.11.2022), Volume 1. Edited by Nchumbonga George Lekelefac

Reverend Father Doctorandus Maurice Akwa: 25th Priestly Anniversary Festschrift (15.11.1997 - 15.11.2022), Volume 1. Edited by Nchumbonga George Lekelefac

Reverend Father Doctorandus Maurice Akwa: 25th Priestly Anniversary Festschrift (15.11.1997 - 15.11.2022), Volume 1. Edited by Nchumbonga George Lekelefac

Reverend Father Doctorandus Maurice Akwa: 25th Priestly Anniversary Festschrift (15.11.1997 - 15.11.2022), Volume 1. Edited by Nchumbonga George Lekelefac

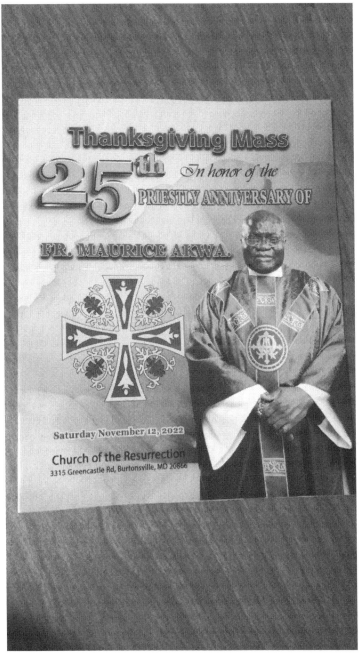

Reverend Father Doctorandus Maurice Akwa: 25th Priestly Anniversary Festschrift (15.11.1997 - 15.11.2022), Volume 1. Edited by Nchumbonga George Lekelefac

Reverend Father Doctorandus Maurice Akwa: 25th Priestly Anniversary Festschrift (15.11.1997 - 15.11.2022), Volume 1. Edited by Nchumbonga George Lekelefac

Reverend Father Doctorandus Maurice Akwa: 25th Priestly Anniversary Festschrift (15.11.1997 - 15.11.2022), Volume 1. Edited by Nchumbonga George Lekelefac

Reverend Father Doctorandus Maurice Akwa: 25th Priestly Anniversary Festschrift (15.11.1997 - 15.11.2022), Volume 1. Edited by Nchumbonga George Lekelefac

Reverend Father Doctorandus Maurice Akwa: 25th Priestly Anniversary Festschrift (15.11.1997 - 15.11.2022), Volume 1. Edited by Nchumbonga George Lekelefac

Reverend Father Doctorandus Maurice Akwa: 25th Priestly Anniversary Festschrift (15.11.1997 - 15.11.2022), Volume 1. Edited by Nchumbonga George Lekelefac

Reverend Father Doctorandus Maurice Akwa: 25th Priestly Anniversary Festschrift (15.11.1997 - 15.11.2022), Volume 1. Edited by Nchumbonga George Lekelefac

Reverend Father Doctorandus Maurice Akwa: 25th Priestly Anniversary Festschrift (15.11.1997 - 15.11.2022), Volume 1. Edited by Nchumbonga George Lekelefac

Reverend Father Doctorandus Maurice Akwa: 25th Priestly Anniversary Festschrift (15.11.1997 - 15.11.2022), Volume 1. Edited by Nchumbonga George Lekelefac

Reverend Father Doctorandus Maurice Akwa: 25th Priestly Anniversary Festschrift
(15.11.1997 - 15.11.2022), Volume 1. Edited by Nchumbonga George Lekelefac

Reverend Father Doctorandus Maurice Akwa: 25th Priestly Anniversary Festschrift (15.11.1997 - 15.11.2022), Volume 1. Edited by Nchumbonga George Lekelefac

Reverend Father Doctorandus Maurice Akwa: 25th Priestly Anniversary Festschrift (15.11.1997 - 15.11.2022), Volume 1. Edited by Nchumbonga George Lekelefac

Reverend Father Doctorandus Maurice Akwa: 25th Priestly Anniversary Festschrift (15.11.1997 - 15.11.2022), Volume 1. Edited by Nchumbonga George Lekelefac

Reverend Father Doctorandus Maurice Akwa: 25th Priestly Anniversary Festschrift (15.11.1997 - 15.11.2022), Volume 1. Edited by Nchumbonga George Lekelefac

Reverend Father Doctorandus Maurice Akwa: 25th Priestly Anniversary Festschrift (15.11.1997 - 15.11.2022), Volume 1. Edited by Nchumbonga George Lekelefac

Reverend Father Doctorandus Maurice Akwa: 25th Priestly Anniversary Festschrift
(15.11.1997 - 15.11.2022), Volume 1. Edited by Nchumbonga George Lekelefac

Reverend Father Doctorandus Maurice Akwa: 25th Priestly Anniversary Festschrift
(15.11.1997 - 15.11.2022), Volume 1. Edited by Nchumbonga George Lekelefac

Reverend Father Doctorandus Maurice Akwa: 25th Priestly Anniversary Festschrift (15.11.1997 - 15.11.2022), Volume 1. Edited by Nchumbonga George Lekelefac

Reverend Father Doctorandus Maurice Akwa: 25th Priestly Anniversary Festschrift
(15.11.1997 - 15.11.2022), Volume 1. Edited by Nchumbonga George Lekelefac

Reverend Father Doctorandus Maurice Akwa: 25th Priestly Anniversary Festschrift (15.11.1997 - 15.11.2022), Volume 1. Edited by Nchumbonga George Lekelefac

Reverend Father Doctorandus Maurice Akwa: 25th Priestly Anniversary Festschrift (15.11.1997 - 15.11.2022), Volume 1. Edited by Nchumbonga George Lekelefac

Reverend Father Doctorandus Maurice Akwa: 25th Priestly Anniversary Festschrift (15.11.1997 - 15.11.2022), Volume 1. Edited by Nchumbonga George Lekelefac

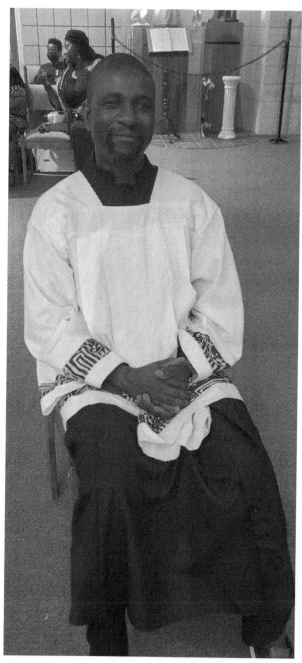

Reverend Father Doctorandus Maurice Akwa: 25th Priestly Anniversary Festschrift (15.11.1997 - 15.11.2022), Volume 1. Edited by Nchumbonga George Lekelefac

Reverend Father Doctorandus Maurice Akwa: 25th Priestly Anniversary Festschrift (15.11.1997 - 15.11.2022), Volume 1. Edited by Nchumbonga George Lekelefac

Reverend Father Doctorandus Maurice Akwa: 25th Priestly Anniversary Festschrift (15.11.1997 - 15.11.2022), Volume 1. Edited by Nchumbonga George Lekelefac

Reverend Father Doctorandus Maurice Akwa: 25th Priestly Anniversary Festschrift (15.11.1997 - 15.11.2022), Volume 1. Edited by Nchumbonga George Lekelefac

Reverend Father Doctorandus Maurice Akwa: 25th Priestly Anniversary Festschrift (15.11.1997 - 15.11.2022), Volume 1. Edited by Nchumbonga George Lekelefac

Reverend Father Doctorandus Maurice Akwa: 25th Priestly Anniversary Festschrift (15.11.1997 - 15.11.2022), Volume 1. Edited by Nchumbonga George Lekelefac

Reverend Father Doctorandus Maurice Akwa: 25th Priestly Anniversary Festschrift (15.11.1997 - 15.11.2022), Volume 1. Edited by Nchumbonga George Lekelefac

Reverend Father Doctorandus Maurice Akwa: 25th Priestly Anniversary Festschrift (15.11.1997 - 15.11.2022), Volume 1. Edited by Nchumbonga George Lekelefac

Reverend Father Doctorandus Maurice Akwa: 25th Priestly Anniversary Festschrift
(15.11.1997 - 15.11.2022), Volume 1. Edited by Nchumbonga George Lekelefac

Reverend Father Doctorandus Maurice Akwa: 25th Priestly Anniversary Festschrift (15.11.1997 - 15.11.2022), Volume 1. Edited by Nchumbonga George Lekelefac

Reverend Father Doctorandus Maurice Akwa: 25th Priestly Anniversary Festschrift (15.11.1997 - 15.11.2022), Volume 1. Edited by Nchumbonga George Lekelefac

Reverend Father Doctorandus Maurice Akwa: 25th Priestly Anniversary Festschrift (15.11.1997 - 15.11.2022), Volume 1. Edited by Nchumbonga George Lekelefac

Reverend Father Doctorandus Maurice Akwa: 25th Priestly Anniversary Festschrift (15.11.1997 - 15.11.2022), Volume 1. Edited by Nchumbonga George Lekelefac

Reverend Father Doctorandus Maurice Akwa: 25th Priestly Anniversary Festschrift (15.11.1997 - 15.11.2022), Volume 1. Edited by Nchumbonga George Lekelefac

Reverend Father Doctorandus Maurice Akwa: 25th Priestly Anniversary Festschrift (15.11.1997 - 15.11.2022), Volume 1. Edited by Nchumbonga George Lekelefac

Reverend Father Doctorandus Maurice Akwa: 25th Priestly Anniversary Festschrift (15.11.1997 - 15.11.2022), Volume 1. Edited by Nchumbonga George Lekelefac

Reverend Father Doctorandus Maurice Akwa: 25th Priestly Anniversary Festschrift (15.11.1997 - 15.11.2022), Volume 1. Edited by Nchumbonga George Lekelefac

Reverend Father Doctorandus Maurice Akwa: 25th Priestly Anniversary Festschrift (15.11.1997 - 15.11.2022), Volume 1. Edited by Nchumbonga George Lekelefac

Reverend Father Doctorandus Maurice Akwa: 25th Priestly Anniversary Festschrift (15.11.1997 - 15.11.2022), Volume 1. Edited by Nchumbonga George Lekelefac

Reverend Father Doctorandus Maurice Akwa: 25th Priestly Anniversary Festschrift (15.11.1997 - 15.11.2022), Volume 1. Edited by Nchumbonga George Lekelefac

Reverend Father Doctorandus Maurice Akwa: 25th Priestly Anniversary Festschrift (15.11.1997 - 15.11.2022), Volume 1. Edited by Nchumbonga George Lekelefac

Reverend Father Doctorandus Maurice Akwa: 25th Priestly Anniversary Festschrift (15.11.1997 - 15.11.2022), Volume 1. Edited by Nchumbonga George Lekelefac

Reverend Father Doctorandus Maurice Akwa: 25th Priestly Anniversary Festschrift (15.11.1997 - 15.11.2022), Volume 1. Edited by Nchumbonga George Lekelefac

Reverend Father Doctorandus Maurice Akwa: 25th Priestly Anniversary Festschrift (15.11.1997 - 15.11.2022), Volume 1. Edited by Nchumbonga George Lekelefac

Reverend Father Doctorandus Maurice Akwa: 25th Priestly Anniversary Festschrift (15.11.1997 - 15.11.2022), Volume 1. Edited by Nchumbonga George Lekelefac

Reverend Father Doctorandus Maurice Akwa: 25th Priestly Anniversary Festschrift (15.11.1997 - 15.11.2022), Volume 1. Edited by Nchumbonga George Lekelefac

Reverend Father Doctorandus Maurice Akwa: 25th Priestly Anniversary Festschrift (15.11.1997 - 15.11.2022), Volume 1. Edited by Nchumbonga George Lekelefac

Reverend Father Doctorandus Maurice Akwa: 25th Priestly Anniversary Festschrift (15.11.1997 - 15.11.2022), Volume 1. Edited by Nchumbonga George Lekelefac

Reverend Father Doctorandus Maurice Akwa: 25th Priestly Anniversary Festschrift (15.11.1997 - 15.11.2022), Volume 1. Edited by Nchumbonga George Lekelefac

Reverend Father Doctorandus Maurice Akwa: 25th Priestly Anniversary Festschrift (15.11.1997 - 15.11.2022), Volume 1. Edited by Nchumbonga George Lekelefac

Reverend Father Doctorandus Maurice Akwa: 25th Priestly Anniversary Festschrift (15.11.1997 - 15.11.2022), Volume 1. Edited by Nchumbonga George Lekelefac

Reverend Father Doctorandus Maurice Akwa: 25th Priestly Anniversary Festschrift (15.11.1997 - 15.11.2022), Volume 1. Edited by Nchumbonga George Lekelefac

Reverend Father Doctorandus Maurice Akwa: 25th Priestly Anniversary Festschrift (15.11.1997 - 15.11.2022), Volume 1. Edited by Nchumbonga George Lekelefac

Chapter Six: Pictures of Thanksgiving Mas son the Occasion of 25th Priestly Anniversary of Fr. Maurice Akwa, St Lawrence Church, 6222 Franconia Rd, Alexandria, VA, USA

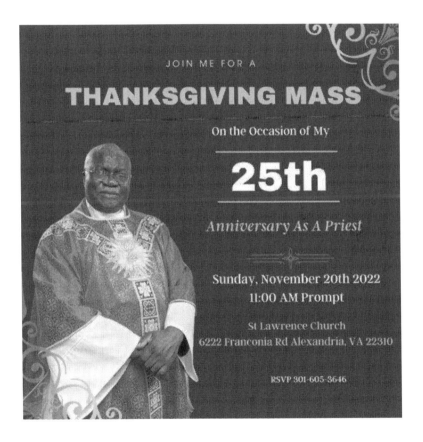

Reverend Father Doctorandus Maurice Akwa: 25th Priestly Anniversary Festschrift (15.11.1997 - 15.11.2022), Volume 1. Edited by Nchumbonga George Lekelefac

Reverend Father Doctorandus Maurice Akwa: 25th Priestly Anniversary Festschrift (15.11.1997 - 15.11.2022), Volume 1. Edited by Nchumbonga George Lekelefac

Reverend Father Doctorandus Maurice Akwa: 25th Priestly Anniversary Festschrift (15.11.1997 - 15.11.2022), Volume 1. Edited by Nchumbonga George Lekelefac

Reverend Father Doctorandus Maurice Akwa: 25th Priestly Anniversary Festschrift (15.11.1997 - 15.11.2022), Volume 1. Edited by Nchumbonga George Lekelefac

Reverend Father Doctorandus Maurice Akwa: 25th Priestly Anniversary Festschrift (15.11.1997 - 15.11.2022), Volume 1. Edited by Nchumbonga George Lekelefac

Reverend Father Doctorandus Maurice Akwa: 25th Priestly Anniversary Festschrift (15.11.1997 - 15.11.2022), Volume 1. Edited by Nchumbonga George Lekelefac

Reverend Father Doctorandus Maurice Akwa: 25th Priestly Anniversary Festschrift (15.11.1997 - 15.11.2022), Volume 1. Edited by Nchumbonga George Lekelefac

Reverend Father Doctorandus Maurice Akwa: 25th Priestly Anniversary Festschrift (15.11.1997 - 15.11.2022), Volume 1. Edited by Nchumbonga George Lekelefac

Reverend Father Doctorandus Maurice Akwa: 25th Priestly Anniversary Festschrift (15.11.1997 - 15.11.2022), Volume 1. Edited by Nchumbonga George Lekelefac

Reverend Father Doctorandus Maurice Akwa: 25th Priestly Anniversary Festschrift (15.11.1997 - 15.11.2022), Volume 1. Edited by Nchumbonga George Lekelefac

Reverend Father Doctorandus Maurice Akwa: 25th Priestly Anniversary Festschrift (15.11.1997 - 15.11.2022), Volume 1. Edited by Nchumbonga George Lekelefac

Reverend Father Doctorandus Maurice Akwa: 25th Priestly Anniversary Festschrift (15.11.1997 - 15.11.2022), Volume 1. Edited by Nchumbonga George Lekelefac

Reverend Father Doctorandus Maurice Akwa: 25th Priestly Anniversary Festschrift (15.11.1997 - 15.11.2022), Volume 1. Edited by Nchumbonga George Lekelefac

Reverend Father Doctorandus Maurice Akwa: 25th Priestly Anniversary Festschrift (15.11.1997 - 15.11.2022), Volume 1. Edited by Nchumbonga George Lekelefac

Reverend Father Doctorandus Maurice Akwa: 25th Priestly Anniversary Festschrift (15.11.1997 - 15.11.2022), Volume 1. Edited by Nchumbonga George Lekelefac

Reverend Father Doctorandus Maurice Akwa: 25th Priestly Anniversary Festschrift (15.11.1997 - 15.11.2022), Volume 1. Edited by Nchumbonga George Lekelefac

Reverend Father Doctorandus Maurice Akwa: 25th Priestly Anniversary Festschrift (15.11.1997 - 15.11.2022), Volume 1. Edited by Nchumbonga George Lekelefac

Reverend Father Doctorandus Maurice Akwa: 25th Priestly Anniversary Festschrift (15.11.1997 - 15.11.2022), Volume 1. Edited by Nchumbonga George Lekelefac

Reverend Father Doctorandus Maurice Akwa: 25th Priestly Anniversary Festschrift (15.11.1997 - 15.11.2022), Volume 1. Edited by Nchumbonga George Lekelefac

Reverend Father Doctorandus Maurice Akwa: 25th Priestly Anniversary Festschrift (15.11.1997 - 15.11.2022), Volume 1. Edited by Nchumbonga George Lekelefac

Reverend Father Doctorandus Maurice Akwa: 25th Priestly Anniversary Festschrift (15.11.1997 - 15.11.2022), Volume 1. Edited by Nchumbonga George Lekelefac

Reverend Father Doctorandus Maurice Akwa: 25th Priestly Anniversary Festschrift (15.11.1997 - 15.11.2022), Volume 1. Edited by Nchumbonga George Lekelefac

Reverend Father Doctorandus Maurice Akwa: 25th Priestly Anniversary Festschrift (15.11.1997 - 15.11.2022), Volume 1. Edited by Nchumbonga George Lekelefac

Reverend Father Doctorandus Maurice Akwa: 25th Priestly Anniversary Festschrift (15.11.1997 - 15.11.2022), Volume 1. Edited by Nchumbonga George Lekelefac

Reverend Father Doctorandus Maurice Akwa: 25th Priestly Anniversary Festschrift (15.11.1997 - 15.11.2022), Volume 1. Edited by Nchumbonga George Lekelefac

Reverend Father Doctorandus Maurice Akwa: 25th Priestly Anniversary Festschrift (15.11.1997 - 15.11.2022), Volume 1. Edited by Nchumbonga George Lekelefac

Reverend Father Doctorandus Maurice Akwa: 25th Priestly Anniversary Festschrift (15.11.1997 - 15.11.2022), Volume 1. Edited by Nchumbonga George Lekelefac

Reverend Father Doctorandus Maurice Akwa: 25th Priestly Anniversary Festschrift (15.11.1997 - 15.11.2022), Volume 1. Edited by Nchumbonga George Lekelefac

Reverend Father Doctorandus Maurice Akwa: 25th Priestly Anniversary Festschrift (15.11.1997 - 15.11.2022), Volume 1. Edited by Nchumbonga George Lekelefac

Reverend Father Doctorandus Maurice Akwa: 25th Priestly Anniversary Festschrift (15.11.1997 - 15.11.2022), Volume 1. Edited by Nchumbonga George Lekelefac

Reverend Father Doctorandus Maurice Akwa: 25th Priestly Anniversary Festschrift (15.11.1997 - 15.11.2022), Volume 1. Edited by Nchumbonga George Lekelefac

Reverend Father Doctorandus Maurice Akwa: 25th Priestly Anniversary Festschrift (15.11.1997 - 15.11.2022), Volume 1. Edited by Nchumbonga George Lekelefac

Reverend Father Doctorandus Maurice Akwa: 25th Priestly Anniversary Festschrift (15.11.1997 - 15.11.2022), Volume 1. Edited by Nchumbonga George Lekelefac

Reverend Father Doctorandus Maurice Akwa: 25th Priestly Anniversary Festschrift (15.11.1997 - 15.11.2022), Volume 1. Edited by Nchumbonga George Lekelefac

Reverend Father Doctorandus Maurice Akwa: 25th Priestly Anniversary Festschrift (15.11.1997 - 15.11.2022), Volume 1. Edited by Nchumbonga George Lekelefac

Reverend Father Doctorandus Maurice Akwa: 25th Priestly Anniversary Festschrift (15.11.1997 - 15.11.2022), Volume 1. Edited by Nchumbonga George Lekelefac

Reverend Father Doctorandus Maurice Akwa: 25th Priestly Anniversary Festschrift (15.11.1997 - 15.11.2022), Volume 1. Edited by Nchumbonga George Lekelefac

Reverend Father Doctorandus Maurice Akwa: 25th Priestly Anniversary Festschrift (15.11.1997 - 15.11.2022), Volume 1. Edited by Nchumbonga George Lekelefac

Reverend Father Doctorandus Maurice Akwa: 25th Priestly Anniversary Festschrift (15.11.1997 - 15.11.2022), Volume 1. Edited by Nchumbonga George Lekelefac

Reverend Father Doctorandus Maurice Akwa: 25th Priestly Anniversary Festschrift (15.11.1997 - 15.11.2022), Volume 1. Edited by Nchumbonga George Lekelefac

Reverend Father Doctorandus Maurice Akwa: 25th Priestly Anniversary Festschrift (15.11.1997 - 15.11.2022), Volume 1. Edited by Nchumbonga George Lekelefac

Reverend Father Doctorandus Maurice Akwa: 25th Priestly Anniversary Festschrift (15.11.1997 - 15.11.2022), Volume 1. Edited by Nchumbonga George Lekelefac

Reverend Father Doctorandus Maurice Akwa: 25th Priestly Anniversary Festschrift (15.11.1997 - 15.11.2022), Volume 1. Edited by Nchumbonga George Lekelefac

Reverend Father Doctorandus Maurice Akwa: 25th Priestly Anniversary Festschrift (15.11.1997 - 15.11.2022), Volume 1. Edited by Nchumbonga George Lekelefac

Reverend Father Doctorandus Maurice Akwa: 25th Priestly Anniversary Festschrift (15.11.1997 - 15.11.2022), Volume 1. Edited by Nchumbonga George Lekelefac

Reverend Father Doctorandus Maurice Akwa: 25th Priestly Anniversary Festschrift (15.11.1997 - 15.11.2022), Volume 1. Edited by Nchumbonga George Lekelefac

Chapter Seven: Other Pictures of Father Maurice Akwa

Reverend Father Doctorandus Maurice Akwa: 25th Priestly Anniversary Festschrift (15.11.1997 - 15.11.2022), Volume 1. Edited by Nchumbonga George Lekelefac

Reverend Father Doctorandus Maurice Akwa: 25th Priestly Anniversary Festschrift (15.11.1997 - 15.11.2022), Volume 1. Edited by Nchumbonga George Lekelefac

Reverend Father Doctorandus Maurice Akwa: 25th Priestly Anniversary Festschrift (15.11.1997 - 15.11.2022), Volume 1. Edited by Nchumbonga George Lekelefac

Reverend Father Doctorandus Maurice Akwa: 25th Priestly Anniversary Festschrift (15.11.1997 - 15.11.2022), Volume 1. Edited by Nchumbonga George Lekelefac

Reverend Father Doctorandus Maurice Akwa: 25th Priestly Anniversary Festschrift (15.11.1997 - 15.11.2022), Volume 1. Edited by Nchumbonga George Lekelefac

Reverend Father Doctorandus Maurice Akwa: 25th Priestly Anniversary Festschrift (15.11.1997 - 15.11.2022), Volume 1. Edited by Nchumbonga George Lekelefac

Reverend Father Doctorandus Maurice Akwa: 25th Priestly Anniversary Festschrift (15.11.1997 - 15.11.2022), Volume 1. Edited by Nchumbonga George Lekelefac

Reverend Father Doctorandus Maurice Akwa: 25th Priestly Anniversary Festschrift
(15.11.1997 - 15.11.2022), Volume 1. Edited by Nchumbonga George Lekelefac

Reverend Father Doctorandus Maurice Akwa: 25th Priestly Anniversary Festschrift (15.11.1997 - 15.11.2022), Volume 1. Edited by Nchumbonga George Lekelefac

Reverend Father Doctorandus Maurice Akwa: 25th Priestly Anniversary Festschrift (15.11.1997 - 15.11.2022), Volume 1. Edited by Nchumbonga George Lekelefac

Reverend Father Doctorandus Maurice Akwa: 25th Priestly Anniversary Festschrift (15.11.1997 - 15.11.2022), Volume 1. Edited by Nchumbonga George Lekelefac

Reverend Father Doctorandus Maurice Akwa: 25th Priestly Anniversary Festschrift (15.11.1997 - 15.11.2022), Volume 1. Edited by Nchumbonga George Lekelefac

Reverend Father Doctorandus Maurice Akwa: 25th Priestly Anniversary Festschrift
(15.11.1997 - 15.11.2022), Volume 1. Edited by Nchumbonga George Lekelefac

Reverend Father Doctorandus Maurice Akwa: 25th Priestly Anniversary Festschrift (15.11.1997 - 15.11.2022), Volume 1. Edited by Nchumbonga George Lekelefac

Reverend Father Doctorandus Maurice Akwa: 25th Priestly Anniversary Festschrift (15.11.1997 - 15.11.2022), Volume 1. Edited by Nchumbonga George Lekelefac

Reverend Father Doctorandus Maurice Akwa: 25th Priestly Anniversary Festschrift (15.11.1997 - 15.11.2022), Volume 1. Edited by Nchumbonga George Lekelefac

Reverend Father Doctorandus Maurice Akwa: 25th Priestly Anniversary Festschrift (15.11.1997 - 15.11.2022), Volume 1. Edited by Nchumbonga George Lekelefac

Reverend Father Doctorandus Maurice Akwa: 25th Priestly Anniversary Festschrift (15.11.1997 - 15.11.2022), Volume 1. Edited by Nchumbonga George Lekelefac

Reverend Father Doctorandus Maurice Akwa: 25th Priestly Anniversary Festschrift (15.11.1997 - 15.11.2022), Volume 1. Edited by Nchumbonga George Lekelefac

Reverend Father Doctorandus Maurice Akwa: 25th Priestly Anniversary Festschrift (15.11.1997 - 15.11.2022), Volume 1. Edited by Nchumbonga George Lekelefac

Reverend Father Doctorandus Maurice Akwa: 25th Priestly Anniversary Festschrift (15.11.1997 - 15.11.2022), Volume 1. Edited by Nchumbonga George Lekelefac

Reverend Father Doctorandus Maurice Akwa: 25th Priestly Anniversary Festschrift (15.11.1997 - 15.11.2022), Volume 1. Edited by Nchumbonga George Lekelefac

Reverend Father Doctorandus Maurice Akwa: 25th Priestly Anniversary Festschrift (15.11.1997 - 15.11.2022), Volume 1. Edited by Nchumbonga George Lekelefac

Reverend Father Doctorandus Maurice Akwa: 25th Priestly Anniversary Festschrift (15.11.1997 - 15.11.2022), Volume 1. Edited by Nchumbonga George Lekelefac

Reverend Father Doctorandus Maurice Akwa: 25th Priestly Anniversary Festschrift (15.11.1997 - 15.11.2022), Volume 1. Edited by Nchumbonga George Lekelefac

Reverend Father Doctorandus Maurice Akwa: 25th Priestly Anniversary Festschrift (15.11.1997 - 15.11.2022), Volume 1. Edited by Nchumbonga George Lekelefac

Reverend Father Doctorandus Maurice Akwa: 25th Priestly Anniversary Festschrift
(15.11.1997 - 15.11.2022), Volume 1. Edited by Nchumbonga George Lekelefac

Reverend Father Doctorandus Maurice Akwa: 25th Priestly Anniversary Festschrift (15.11.1997 - 15.11.2022), Volume 1. Edited by Nchumbonga George Lekelefac

Reverend Father Doctorandus Maurice Akwa: 25th Priestly Anniversary Festschrift (15.11.1997 - 15.11.2022), Volume 1. Edited by Nchumbonga George Lekelefac

Reverend Father Doctorandus Maurice Akwa: 25th Priestly Anniversary Festschrift (15.11.1997 - 15.11.2022), Volume 1. Edited by Nchumbonga George Lekelefac

Reverend Father Doctorandus Maurice Akwa: 25th Priestly Anniversary Festschrift (15.11.1997 - 15.11.2022), Volume 1. Edited by Nchumbonga George Lekelefac

Reverend Father Doctorandus Maurice Akwa: 25th Priestly Anniversary Festschrift (15.11.1997 - 15.11.2022), Volume 1. Edited by Nchumbonga George Lekelefac

Reverend Father Doctorandus Maurice Akwa: 25th Priestly Anniversary Festschrift (15.11.1997 - 15.11.2022), Volume 1. Edited by Nchumbonga George Lekelefac

Reverend Father Doctorandus Maurice Akwa: 25th Priestly Anniversary Festschrift (15.11.1997 - 15.11.2022), Volume 1. Edited by Nchumbonga George Lekelefac

Reverend Father Doctorandus Maurice Akwa: 25th Priestly Anniversary Festschrift (15.11.1997 - 15.11.2022), Volume 1. Edited by Nchumbonga George Lekelefac

Reverend Father Doctorandus Maurice Akwa: 25th Priestly Anniversary Festschrift (15.11.1997 - 15.11.2022), Volume 1. Edited by Nchumbonga George Lekelefac

Reverend Father Doctorandus Maurice Akwa: 25th Priestly Anniversary Festschrift (15.11.1997 - 15.11.2022), Volume 1. Edited by Nchumbonga George Lekelefac

Reverend Father Doctorandus Maurice Akwa: 25th Priestly Anniversary Festschrift (15.11.1997 - 15.11.2022), Volume 1. Edited by Nchumbonga George Lekelefac

Reverend Father Doctorandus Maurice Akwa: 25th Priestly Anniversary Festschrift (15.11.1997 - 15.11.2022), Volume 1. Edited by Nchumbonga George Lekelefac

Reverend Father Doctorandus Maurice Akwa: 25th Priestly Anniversary Festschrift (15.11.1997 - 15.11.2022), Volume 1. Edited by Nchumbonga George Lekelefac

Reverend Father Doctorandus Maurice Akwa: 25th Priestly Anniversary Festschrift (15.11.1997 - 15.11.2022), Volume 1. Edited by Nchumbonga George Lekelefac

Reverend Father Doctorandus Maurice Akwa: 25th Priestly Anniversary Festschrift (15.11.1997 - 15.11.2022), Volume 1. Edited by Nchumbonga George Lekelefac

Reverend Father Doctorandus Maurice Akwa: 25th Priestly Anniversary Festschrift (15.11.1997 - 15.11.2022), Volume 1. Edited by Nchumbonga George Lekelefac

Reverend Father Doctorandus Maurice Akwa: 25th Priestly Anniversary Festschrift (15.11.1997 - 15.11.2022), Volume 1. Edited by Nchumbonga George Lekelefac

Reverend Father Doctorandus Maurice Akwa: 25th Priestly Anniversary Festschrift (15.11.1997 - 15.11.2022), Volume 1. Edited by Nchumbonga George Lekelefac

Reverend Father Doctorandus Maurice Akwa: 25th Priestly Anniversary Festschrift (15.11.1997 - 15.11.2022), Volume 1. Edited by Nchumbonga George Lekelefac

Reverend Father Doctorandus Maurice Akwa: 25th Priestly Anniversary Festschrift (15.11.1997 - 15.11.2022), Volume 1. Edited by Nchumbonga George Lekelefac

Reverend Father Doctorandus Maurice Akwa: 25th Priestly Anniversary Festschrift (15.11.1997 - 15.11.2022), Volume 1. Edited by Nchumbonga George Lekelefac

Reverend Father Doctorandus Maurice Akwa: 25th Priestly Anniversary Festschrift (15.11.1997 - 15.11.2022), Volume 1. Edited by Nchumbonga George Lekelefac

Reverend Father Doctorandus Maurice Akwa: 25th Priestly Anniversary Festschrift (15.11.1997 - 15.11.2022), Volume 1. Edited by Nchumbonga George Lekelefac

Reverend Father Doctorandus Maurice Akwa: 25th Priestly Anniversary Festschrift (15.11.1997 - 15.11.2022), Volume 1. Edited by Nchumbonga George Lekelefac

Reverend Father Doctorandus Maurice Akwa: 25th Priestly Anniversary Festschrift (15.11.1997 - 15.11.2022), Volume 1. Edited by Nchumbonga George Lekelefac

Reverend Father Doctorandus Maurice Akwa: 25th Priestly Anniversary Festschrift (15.11.1997 - 15.11.2022), Volume 1. Edited by Nchumbonga George Lekelefac

Bishop Michael Burbidge before whom I renewed my Sacerdotal Promises today.
Thanks for all your prayers and encouragements in my ministry.

Reverend Father Doctorandus Maurice Akwa: 25th Priestly Anniversary Festschrift (15.11.1997 - 15.11.2022), Volume 1. Edited by Nchumbonga George Lekelefac

Reverend Father Doctorandus Maurice Akwa: 25th Priestly Anniversary Festschrift (15.11.1997 - 15.11.2022), Volume 1. Edited by Nchumbonga George Lekelefac

Reverend Father Doctorandus Maurice Akwa: 25th Priestly Anniversary Festschrift (15.11.1997 - 15.11.2022), Volume 1. Edited by Nchumbonga George Lekelefac

Reverend Father Doctorandus Maurice Akwa: 25th Priestly Anniversary Festschrift (15.11.1997 - 15.11.2022), Volume 1. Edited by Nchumbonga George Lekelefac

Reverend Father Doctorandus Maurice Akwa: 25th Priestly Anniversary Festschrift (15.11.1997 - 15.11.2022), Volume 1. Edited by Nchumbonga George Lekelefac

Reverend Father Doctorandus Maurice Akwa: 25th Priestly Anniversary Festschrift (15.11.1997 - 15.11.2022), Volume 1. Edited by Nchumbonga George Lekelefac

Reverend Father Doctorandus Maurice Akwa: 25th Priestly Anniversary Festschrift (15.11.1997 - 15.11.2022), Volume 1. Edited by Nchumbonga George Lekelefac

Reverend Father Doctorandus Maurice Akwa: 25th Priestly Anniversary Festschrift (15.11.1997 - 15.11.2022), Volume 1. Edited by Nchumbonga George Lekelefac

Reverend Father Doctorandus Maurice Akwa: 25th Priestly Anniversary Festschrift (15.11.1997 - 15.11.2022), Volume 1. Edited by Nchumbonga George Lekelefac

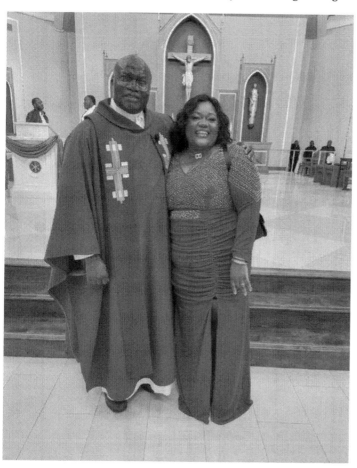

Reverend Father Doctorandus Maurice Akwa: 25th Priestly Anniversary Festschrift (15.11.1997 - 15.11.2022), Volume 1. Edited by Nchumbonga George Lekelefac

Reverend Father Doctorandus Maurice Akwa: 25th Priestly Anniversary Festschrift (15.11.1997 - 15.11.2022), Volume 1. Edited by Nchumbonga George Lekelefac

Reverend Father Doctorandus Maurice Akwa: 25th Priestly Anniversary Festschrift (15.11.1997 - 15.11.2022), Volume 1. Edited by Nchumbonga George Lekelefac

Reverend Father Doctorandus Maurice Akwa: 25th Priestly Anniversary Festschrift (15.11.1997 - 15.11.2022), Volume 1. Edited by Nchumbonga George Lekelefac

Reverend Father Doctorandus Maurice Akwa: 25th Priestly Anniversary Festschrift (15.11.1997 - 15.11.2022), Volume 1. Edited by Nchumbonga George Lekelefac

Reverend Father Doctorandus Maurice Akwa: 25th Priestly Anniversary Festschrift (15.11.1997 - 15.11.2022), Volume 1. Edited by Nchumbonga George Lekelefac

Reverend Father Doctorandus Maurice Akwa: 25th Priestly Anniversary Festschrift (15.11.1997 - 15.11.2022), Volume 1. Edited by Nchumbonga George Lekelefac

Reverend Father Doctorandus Maurice Akwa: 25th Priestly Anniversary Festschrift (15.11.1997 - 15.11.2022), Volume 1. Edited by Nchumbonga George Lekelefac

Reverend Father Doctorandus Maurice Akwa: 25th Priestly Anniversary Festschrift (15.11.1997 - 15.11.2022), Volume 1. Edited by Nchumbonga George Lekelefac

Reverend Father Doctorandus Maurice Akwa: 25th Priestly Anniversary Festschrift (15.11.1997 - 15.11.2022), Volume 1. Edited by Nchumbonga George Lekelefac

Reverend Father Doctorandus Maurice Akwa: 25th Priestly Anniversary Festschrift (15.11.1997 - 15.11.2022), Volume 1. Edited by Nchumbonga George Lekelefac

Reverend Father Doctorandus Maurice Akwa: 25th Priestly Anniversary Festschrift (15.11.1997 - 15.11.2022), Volume 1. Edited by Nchumbonga George Lekelefac

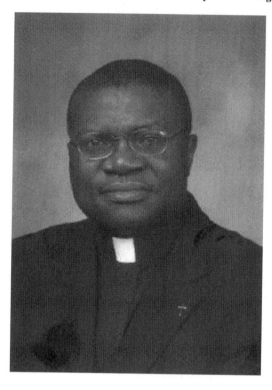

Reverend Father Doctorandus Maurice Akwa: 25th Priestly Anniversary Festschrift (15.11.1997 - 15.11.2022), Volume 1. Edited by Nchumbonga George Lekelefac

Reverend Father Doctorandus Maurice Akwa: 25th Priestly Anniversary Festschrift (15.11.1997 - 15.11.2022), Volume 1. Edited by Nchumbonga George Lekelefac

Reverend Father Doctorandus Maurice Akwa: 25th Priestly Anniversary Festschrift (15.11.1997 - 15.11.2022), Volume 1. Edited by Nchumbonga George Lekelefac

Reverend Father Doctorandus Maurice Akwa: 25th Priestly Anniversary Festschrift (15.11.1997 - 15.11.2022), Volume 1. Edited by Nchumbonga George Lekelefac

Reverend Father Doctorandus Maurice Akwa: 25th Priestly Anniversary Festschrift (15.11.1997 - 15.11.2022), Volume 1. Edited by Nchumbonga George Lekelefac

Reverend Father Doctorandus Maurice Akwa: 25th Priestly Anniversary Festschrift (15.11.1997 - 15.11.2022), Volume 1. Edited by Nchumbonga George Lekelefac

Reverend Father Doctorandus Maurice Akwa: 25th Priestly Anniversary Festschrift (15.11.1997 - 15.11.2022), Volume 1. Edited by Nchumbonga George Lekelefac

Reverend Father Doctorandus Maurice Akwa: 25th Priestly Anniversary Festschrift (15.11.1997 - 15.11.2022), Volume 1. Edited by Nchumbonga George Lekelefac

Reverend Father Doctorandus Maurice Akwa: 25th Priestly Anniversary Festschrift (15.11.1997 - 15.11.2022), Volume 1. Edited by Nchumbonga George Lekelefac

Reverend Father Doctorandus Maurice Akwa: 25th Priestly Anniversary Festschrift (15.11.1997 - 15.11.2022), Volume 1. Edited by Nchumbonga George Lekelefac

I SAW THE JESUS IN HIM

Reverend Father Doctorandus Maurice Akwa: 25th Priestly Anniversary Festschrift (15.11.1997 - 15.11.2022), Volume 1. Edited by Nchumbonga George Lekelefac

Reverend Father Doctorandus Maurice Akwa: 25th Priestly Anniversary Festschrift (15.11.1997 - 15.11.2022), Volume 1. Edited by Nchumbonga George Lekelefac

Reverend Father Doctorandus Maurice Akwa: 25th Priestly Anniversary Festschrift (15.11.1997 - 15.11.2022), Volume 1. Edited by Nchumbonga George Lekelefac

Reverend Father Doctorandus Maurice Akwa: 25th Priestly Anniversary Festschrift (15.11.1997 - 15.11.2022), Volume 1. Edited by Nchumbonga George Lekelefac

Reverend Father Doctorandus Maurice Akwa: 25th Priestly Anniversary Festschrift (15.11.1997 - 15.11.2022), Volume 1. Edited by Nchumbonga George Lekelefac

Reverend Father Doctorandus Maurice Akwa: 25th Priestly Anniversary Festschrift (15.11.1997 - 15.11.2022), Volume 1. Edited by Nchumbonga George Lekelefac

Reverend Father Doctorandus Maurice Akwa: 25th Priestly Anniversary Festschrift (15.11.1997 - 15.11.2022), Volume 1. Edited by Nchumbonga George Lekelefac

Reverend Father Doctorandus Maurice Akwa: 25th Priestly Anniversary Festschrift (15.11.1997 - 15.11.2022), Volume 1. Edited by Nchumbonga George Lekelefac

Reverend Father Doctorandus Maurice Akwa: 25th Priestly Anniversary Festschrift (15.11.1997 - 15.11.2022), Volume 1. Edited by Nchumbonga George Lekelefac

Reverend Father Doctorandus Maurice Akwa: 25th Priestly Anniversary Festschrift (15.11.1997 - 15.11.2022), Volume 1. Edited by Nchumbonga George Lekelefac

Reverend Father Doctorandus Maurice Akwa: 25th Priestly Anniversary Festschrift (15.11.1997 - 15.11.2022), Volume 1. Edited by Nchumbonga George Lekelefac

Reverend Father Doctorandus Maurice Akwa: 25th Priestly Anniversary Festschrift (15.11.1997 - 15.11.2022), Volume 1. Edited by Nchumbonga George Lekelefac

Reverend Father Doctorandus Maurice Akwa: 25th Priestly Anniversary Festschrift
(15.11.1997 - 15.11.2022), Volume 1. Edited by Nchumbonga George Lekelefac

Reverend Father Doctorandus Maurice Akwa: 25th Priestly Anniversary Festschrift (15.11.1997 - 15.11.2022), Volume 1. Edited by Nchumbonga George Lekelefac

Reverend Father Doctorandus Maurice Akwa: 25th Priestly Anniversary Festschrift (15.11.1997 - 15.11.2022), Volume 1. Edited by Nchumbonga George Lekelefac

Reverend Father Doctorandus Maurice Akwa: 25th Priestly Anniversary Festschrift (15.11.1997 - 15.11.2022), Volume 1. Edited by Nchumbonga George Lekelefac

Reverend Father Doctorandus Maurice Akwa: 25th Priestly Anniversary Festschrift (15.11.1997 - 15.11.2022), Volume 1. Edited by Nchumbonga George Lekelefac

Reverend Father Doctorandus Maurice Akwa: 25th Priestly Anniversary Festschrift (15.11.1997 - 15.11.2022), Volume 1. Edited by Nchumbonga George Lekelefac

Reverend Father Doctorandus Maurice Akwa: 25th Priestly Anniversary Festschrift (15.11.1997 - 15.11.2022), Volume 1. Edited by Nchumbonga George Lekelefac

Reverend Father Doctorandus Maurice Akwa: 25th Priestly Anniversary Festschrift (15.11.1997 - 15.11.2022), Volume 1. Edited by Nchumbonga George Lekelefac

Reverend Father Doctorandus Maurice Akwa: 25th Priestly Anniversary Festschrift (15.11.1997 - 15.11.2022), Volume 1. Edited by Nchumbonga George Lekelefac

Reverend Father Doctorandus Maurice Akwa: 25th Priestly Anniversary Festschrift (15.11.1997 - 15.11.2022), Volume 1. Edited by Nchumbonga George Lekelefac

Reverend Father Doctorandus Maurice Akwa: 25th Priestly Anniversary Festschrift (15.11.1997 - 15.11.2022), Volume 1. Edited by Nchumbonga George Lekelefac

Reverend Father Doctorandus Maurice Akwa: 25th Priestly Anniversary Festschrift (15.11.1997 - 15.11.2022), Volume 1. Edited by Nchumbonga George Lekelefac

Reverend Father Doctorandus Maurice Akwa: 25th Priestly Anniversary Festschrift (15.11.1997 - 15.11.2022), Volume 1. Edited by Nchumbonga George Lekelefac

Reverend Father Doctorandus Maurice Akwa: 25th Priestly Anniversary Festschrift (15.11.1997 - 15.11.2022), Volume 1. Edited by Nchumbonga George Lekelefac

Reverend Father Doctorandus Maurice Akwa: 25th Priestly Anniversary Festschrift (15.11.1997 - 15.11.2022), Volume 1. Edited by Nchumbonga George Lekelefac

Reverend Father Doctorandus Maurice Akwa: 25th Priestly Anniversary Festschrift (15.11.1997 - 15.11.2022), Volume 1. Edited by Nchumbonga George Lekelefac

Reverend Father Doctorandus Maurice Akwa: 25th Priestly Anniversary Festschrift (15.11.1997 - 15.11.2022), Volume 1. Edited by Nchumbonga George Lekelefac

Reverend Father Doctorandus Maurice Akwa: 25th Priestly Anniversary Festschrift (15.11.1997 - 15.11.2022), Volume 1. Edited by Nchumbonga George Lekelefac

Reverend Father Doctorandus Maurice Akwa: 25th Priestly Anniversary Festschrift (15.11.1997 - 15.11.2022), Volume 1. Edited by Nchumbonga George Lekelefac

Reverend Father Doctorandus Maurice Akwa: 25th Priestly Anniversary Festschrift (15.11.1997 - 15.11.2022), Volume 1. Edited by Nchumbonga George Lekelefac

Reverend Father Doctorandus Maurice Akwa: 25th Priestly Anniversary Festschrift (15.11.1997 - 15.11.2022), Volume 1. Edited by Nchumbonga George Lekelefac

Reverend Father Doctorandus Maurice Akwa: 25th Priestly Anniversary Festschrift
(15.11.1997 - 15.11.2022), Volume 1. Edited by Nchumbonga George Lekelefac

Reverend Father Doctorandus Maurice Akwa: 25th Priestly Anniversary Festschrift (15.11.1997 - 15.11.2022), Volume 1. Edited by Nchumbonga George Lekelefac

Reverend Father Doctorandus Maurice Akwa: 25th Priestly Anniversary Festschrift (15.11.1997 - 15.11.2022), Volume 1. Edited by Nchumbonga George Lekelefac

Reverend Father Doctorandus Maurice Akwa: 25th Priestly Anniversary Festschrift (15.11.1997 - 15.11.2022), Volume 1. Edited by Nchumbonga George Lekelefac

Reverend Father Doctorandus Maurice Akwa: 25th Priestly Anniversary Festschrift (15.11.1997 - 15.11.2022), Volume 1. Edited by Nchumbonga George Lekelefac

Reverend Father Doctorandus Maurice Akwa: 25th Priestly Anniversary Festschrift (15.11.1997 - 15.11.2022), Volume 1. Edited by Nchumbonga George Lekelefac

Reverend Father Doctorandus Maurice Akwa: 25th Priestly Anniversary Festschrift (15.11.1997 - 15.11.2022), Volume 1. Edited by Nchumbonga George Lekelefac

Reverend Father Doctorandus Maurice Akwa: 25th Priestly Anniversary Festschrift (15.11.1997 - 15.11.2022), Volume 1. Edited by Nchumbonga George Lekelefac

Reverend Father Doctorandus Maurice Akwa: 25th Priestly Anniversary Festschrift (15.11.1997 - 15.11.2022), Volume 1. Edited by Nchumbonga George Lekelefac

Reverend Father Doctorandus Maurice Akwa: 25th Priestly Anniversary Festschrift (15.11.1997 - 15.11.2022), Volume 1. Edited by Nchumbonga George Lekelefac

Reverend Father Doctorandus Maurice Akwa: 25th Priestly Anniversary Festschrift (15.11.1997 - 15.11.2022), Volume 1. Edited by Nchumbonga George Lekelefac

Reverend Father Doctorandus Maurice Akwa: 25th Priestly Anniversary Festschrift (15.11.1997 - 15.11.2022), Volume 1. Edited by Nchumbonga George Lekelefac

Reverend Father Doctorandus Maurice Akwa: 25th Priestly Anniversary Festschrift
(15.11.1997 - 15.11.2022), Volume 1. Edited by Nchumbonga George Lekelefac

Reverend Father Doctorandus Maurice Akwa: 25th Priestly Anniversary Festschrift (15.11.1997 - 15.11.2022), Volume 1. Edited by Nchumbonga George Lekelefac

Reverend Father Doctorandus Maurice Akwa: 25th Priestly Anniversary Festschrift (15.11.1997 - 15.11.2022), Volume 1. Edited by Nchumbonga George Lekelefac

Reverend Father Doctorandus Maurice Akwa: 25th Priestly Anniversary Festschrift (15.11.1997 - 15.11.2022), Volume 1. Edited by Nchumbonga George Lekelefac

Reverend Father Doctorandus Maurice Akwa: 25th Priestly Anniversary Festschrift (15.11.1997 - 15.11.2022), Volume 1. Edited by Nchumbonga George Lekelefac

Reverend Father Doctorandus Maurice Akwa: 25th Priestly Anniversary Festschrift (15.11.1997 - 15.11.2022), Volume 1. Edited by Nchumbonga George Lekelefac

Reverend Father Doctorandus Maurice Akwa: 25th Priestly Anniversary Festschrift (15.11.1997 - 15.11.2022), Volume 1. Edited by Nchumbonga George Lekelefac

Reverend Father Doctorandus Maurice Akwa: 25th Priestly Anniversary Festschrift (15.11.1997 - 15.11.2022), Volume 1. Edited by Nchumbonga George Lekelefac

Reverend Father Doctorandus Maurice Akwa: 25th Priestly Anniversary Festschrift (15.11.1997 - 15.11.2022), Volume 1. Edited by Nchumbonga George Lekelefac

Reverend Father Doctorandus Maurice Akwa: 25th Priestly Anniversary Festschrift (15.11.1997 - 15.11.2022), Volume 1. Edited by Nchumbonga George Lekelefac

Reverend Father Doctorandus Maurice Akwa: 25th Priestly Anniversary Festschrift (15.11.1997 - 15.11.2022), Volume 1. Edited by Nchumbonga George Lekelefac

Reverend Father Doctorandus Maurice Akwa: 25th Priestly Anniversary Festschrift (15.11.1997 - 15.11.2022), Volume 1. Edited by Nchumbonga George Lekelefac

Reverend Father Doctorandus Maurice Akwa: 25th Priestly Anniversary Festschrift (15.11.1997 - 15.11.2022), Volume 1. Edited by Nchumbonga George Lekelefac

Reverend Father Doctorandus Maurice Akwa: 25th Priestly Anniversary Festschrift (15.11.1997 - 15.11.2022), Volume 1. Edited by Nchumbonga George Lekelefac

Reverend Father Doctorandus Maurice Akwa: 25th Priestly Anniversary Festschrift (15.11.1997 - 15.11.2022), Volume 1. Edited by Nchumbonga George Lekelefac

Reverend Father Doctorandus Maurice Akwa: 25th Priestly Anniversary Festschrift (15.11.1997 - 15.11.2022), Volume 1. Edited by Nchumbonga George Lekelefac

Reverend Father Doctorandus Maurice Akwa: 25th Priestly Anniversary Festschrift (15.11.1997 - 15.11.2022), Volume 1. Edited by Nchumbonga George Lekelefac

Reverend Father Doctorandus Maurice Akwa: 25th Priestly Anniversary Festschrift (15.11.1997 - 15.11.2022), Volume 1. Edited by Nchumbonga George Lekelefac

Reverend Father Doctorandus Maurice Akwa: 25th Priestly Anniversary Festschrift (15.11.1997 - 15.11.2022), Volume 1. Edited by Nchumbonga George Lekelefac

Reverend Father Doctorandus Maurice Akwa: 25th Priestly Anniversary Festschrift (15.11.1997 - 15.11.2022), Volume 1. Edited by Nchumbonga George Lekelefac

Reverend Father Doctorandus Maurice Akwa: 25th Priestly Anniversary Festschrift (15.11.1997 - 15.11.2022), Volume 1. Edited by Nchumbonga George Lekelefac

Reverend Father Doctorandus Maurice Akwa: 25th Priestly Anniversary Festschrift (15.11.1997 - 15.11.2022), Volume 1. Edited by Nchumbonga George Lekelefac

Reverend Father Doctorandus Maurice Akwa: 25th Priestly Anniversary Festschrift (15.11.1997 - 15.11.2022), Volume 1. Edited by Nchumbonga George Lekelefac

Reverend Father Doctorandus Maurice Akwa: 25th Priestly Anniversary Festschrift (15.11.1997 - 15.11.2022), Volume 1. Edited by Nchumbonga George Lekelefac

Reverend Father Doctorandus Maurice Akwa: 25th Priestly Anniversary Festschrift (15.11.1997 - 15.11.2022), Volume 1. Edited by Nchumbonga George Lekelefac

Reverend Father Doctorandus Maurice Akwa: 25th Priestly Anniversary Festschrift (15.11.1997 - 15.11.2022), Volume 1. Edited by Nchumbonga George Lekelefac

Reverend Father Doctorandus Maurice Akwa: 25th Priestly Anniversary Festschrift
(15.11.1997 - 15.11.2022), Volume 1. Edited by Nchumbonga George Lekelefac

septembre 2011

1 jeudi	2 vendredi	3 samedi	4 dimanche	5 lundi	6 mardi
7 mercredi	8 jeudi	9 vendredi	10 samedi	11 dimanche	12 lundi
13 mardi	14 mercredi	15 jeudi	16 vendredi	17 samedi	
18 dimanche	19 lundi	20 mardi	21 mercredi	22 jeudi	
	23 vendredi		24 samedi	25 dimanche	
26 lundi	27 mardi	28 mercredi	29 jeudi	30 vendredi	

Reverend Father Doctorandus Maurice Akwa: 25th Priestly Anniversary Festschrift (15.11.1997 - 15.11.2022), Volume 1. Edited by Nchumbonga George Lekelefac

Reverend Father Doctorandus Maurice Akwa: 25th Priestly Anniversary Festschrift
(15.11.1997 - 15.11.2022), Volume 1. Edited by Nchumbonga George Lekelefac

September 2011

Reverend Father Doctorandus Maurice Akwa: 25th Priestly Anniversary Festschrift (15.11.1997 - 15.11.2022), Volume 1. Edited by Nchumbonga George Lekelefac

Reverend Father Doctorandus Maurice Akwa: 25th Priestly Anniversary Festschrift (15.11.1997 - 15.11.2022), Volume 1. Edited by Nchumbonga George Lekelefac

Reverend Father Doctorandus Maurice Akwa: 25th Priestly Anniversary Festschrift (15.11.1997 - 15.11.2022), Volume 1. Edited by Nchumbonga George Lekelefac

Reverend Father Doctorandus Maurice Akwa: 25th Priestly Anniversary Festschrift (15.11.1997 - 15.11.2022), Volume 1. Edited by Nchumbonga George Lekelefac

Reverend Father Doctorandus Maurice Akwa: 25th Priestly Anniversary Festschrift (15.11.1997 - 15.11.2022), Volume 1. Edited by Nchumbonga George Lekelefac

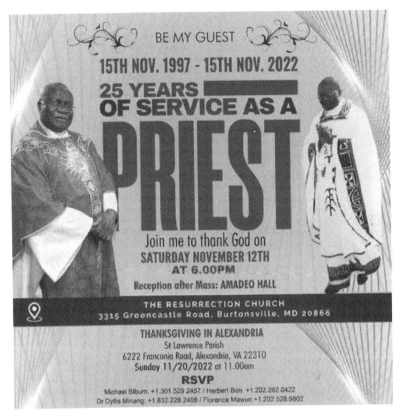

Reverend Father Doctorandus Maurice Akwa: 25th Priestly Anniversary Festschrift (15.11.1997 - 15.11.2022), Volume 1. Edited by Nchumbonga George Lekelefac

11 years ago, as formator faculty at the Major Seminary in Bertoua.

Reverend Father Doctorandus Maurice Akwa: 25th Priestly Anniversary Festschrift (15.11.1997 - 15.11.2022), Volume 1. Edited by Nchumbonga George Lekelefac

Reverend Father Doctorandus Maurice Akwa: 25th Priestly Anniversary Festschrift (15.11.1997 - 15.11.2022), Volume 1. Edited by Nchumbonga George Lekelefac

Reverend Father Doctorandus Maurice Akwa: 25th Priestly Anniversary Festschrift (15.11.1997 - 15.11.2022), Volume 1. Edited by Nchumbonga George Lekelefac

Reverend Father Doctorandus Maurice Akwa: 25th Priestly Anniversary Festschrift (15.11.1997 - 15.11.2022), Volume 1. Edited by Nchumbonga George Lekelefac

Reverend Father Doctorandus Maurice Akwa: 25th Priestly Anniversary Festschrift (15.11.1997 - 15.11.2022), Volume 1. Edited by Nchumbonga George Lekelefac

Reverend Father Doctorandus Maurice Akwa: 25th Priestly Anniversary Festschrift (15.11.1997 - 15.11.2022), Volume 1. Edited by Nchumbonga George Lekelefac

Reverend Father Doctorandus Maurice Akwa: 25th Priestly Anniversary Festschrift (15.11.1997 - 15.11.2022), Volume 1. Edited by Nchumbonga George Lekelefac

Reverend Father Doctorandus Maurice Akwa: 25th Priestly Anniversary Festschrift (15.11.1997 - 15.11.2022), Volume 1. Edited by Nchumbonga George Lekelefac

Reverend Father Doctorandus Maurice Akwa: 25th Priestly Anniversary Festschrift (15.11.1997 - 15.11.2022), Volume 1. Edited by Nchumbonga George Lekelefac

Reverend Father Doctorandus Maurice Akwa: 25th Priestly Anniversary Festschrift (15.11.1997 - 15.11.2022), Volume 1. Edited by Nchumbonga George Lekelefac

Reverend Father Doctorandus Maurice Akwa: 25th Priestly Anniversary Festschrift (15.11.1997 - 15.11.2022), Volume 1. Edited by Nchumbonga George Lekelefac

Reverend Father Doctorandus Maurice Akwa: 25th Priestly Anniversary Festschrift (15.11.1997 - 15.11.2022), Volume 1. Edited by Nchumbonga George Lekelefac

Reverend Father Doctorandus Maurice Akwa: 25th Priestly Anniversary Festschrift (15.11.1997 - 15.11.2022), Volume 1. Edited by Nchumbonga George Lekelefac

Reverend Father Doctorandus Maurice Akwa: 25th Priestly Anniversary Festschrift (15.11.1997 - 15.11.2022), Volume 1. Edited by Nchumbonga George Lekelefac

Reverend Father Doctorandus Maurice Akwa: 25th Priestly Anniversary Festschrift (15.11.1997 - 15.11.2022), Volume 1. Edited by Nchumbonga George Lekelefac

Reverend Father Doctorandus Maurice Akwa: 25th Priestly Anniversary Festschrift (15.11.1997 - 15.11.2022), Volume 1. Edited by Nchumbonga George Lekelefac

Reverend Father Doctorandus Maurice Akwa: 25th Priestly Anniversary Festschrift (15.11.1997 - 15.11.2022), Volume 1. Edited by Nchumbonga George Lekelefac

Reverend Father Doctorandus Maurice Akwa: 25th Priestly Anniversary Festschrift (15.11.1997 - 15.11.2022), Volume 1. Edited by Nchumbonga George Lekelefac

Reverend Father Doctorandus Maurice Akwa: 25th Priestly Anniversary Festschrift (15.11.1997 - 15.11.2022), Volume 1. Edited by Nchumbonga George Lekelefac

Reverend Father Doctorandus Maurice Akwa: 25th Priestly Anniversary Festschrift (15.11.1997 - 15.11.2022), Volume 1. Edited by Nchumbonga George Lekelefac

Reverend Father Doctorandus Maurice Akwa: 25th Priestly Anniversary Festschrift (15.11.1997 - 15.11.2022), Volume 1. Edited by Nchumbonga George Lekelefac

Reverend Father Doctorandus Maurice Akwa: 25th Priestly Anniversary Festschrift (15.11.1997 - 15.11.2022), Volume 1. Edited by Nchumbonga George Lekelefac

Reverend Father Doctorandus Maurice Akwa: 25th Priestly Anniversary Festschrift (15.11.1997 - 15.11.2022), Volume 1. Edited by Nchumbonga George Lekelefac

Reverend Father Doctorandus Maurice Akwa: 25th Priestly Anniversary Festschrift (15.11.1997 - 15.11.2022), Volume 1. Edited by Nchumbonga George Lekelefac

Reverend Father Doctorandus Maurice Akwa: 25th Priestly Anniversary Festschrift (15.11.1997 - 15.11.2022), Volume 1. Edited by Nchumbonga George Lekelefac

Reverend Father Doctorandus Maurice Akwa: 25th Priestly Anniversary Festschrift (15.11.1997 - 15.11.2022), Volume 1. Edited by Nchumbonga George Lekelefac

Reverend Father Doctorandus Maurice Akwa: 25th Priestly Anniversary Festschrift (15.11.1997 - 15.11.2022), Volume 1. Edited by Nchumbonga George Lekelefac

Reverend Father Doctorandus Maurice Akwa: 25th Priestly Anniversary Festschrift (15.11.1997 - 15.11.2022), Volume 1. Edited by Nchumbonga George Lekelefac

Reverend Father Doctorandus Maurice Akwa: 25th Priestly Anniversary Festschrift (15.11.1997 - 15.11.2022), Volume 1. Edited by Nchumbonga George Lekelefac

Reverend Father Doctorandus Maurice Akwa: 25th Priestly Anniversary Festschrift (15.11.1997 - 15.11.2022), Volume 1. Edited by Nchumbonga George Lekelefac

Reverend Father Doctorandus Maurice Akwa: 25th Priestly Anniversary Festschrift (15.11.1997 - 15.11.2022), Volume 1. Edited by Nchumbonga George Lekelefac

Reverend Father Doctorandus Maurice Akwa: 25th Priestly Anniversary Festschrift (15.11.1997 - 15.11.2022), Volume 1. Edited by Nchumbonga George Lekelefac

Reverend Father Doctorandus Maurice Akwa: 25th Priestly Anniversary Festschrift (15.11.1997 - 15.11.2022), Volume 1. Edited by Nchumbonga George Lekelefac

Reverend Father Doctorandus Maurice Akwa: 25th Priestly Anniversary Festschrift (15.11.1997 - 15.11.2022), Volume 1. Edited by Nchumbonga George Lekelefac

Reverend Father Doctorandus Maurice Akwa: 25th Priestly Anniversary Festschrift (15.11.1997 - 15.11.2022), Volume 1. Edited by Nchumbonga George Lekelefac

Reverend Father Doctorandus Maurice Akwa: 25th Priestly Anniversary Festschrift (15.11.1997 - 15.11.2022), Volume 1. Edited by Nchumbonga George Lekelefac

Reverend Father Doctorandus Maurice Akwa: 25th Priestly Anniversary Festschrift (15.11.1997 - 15.11.2022), Volume 1. Edited by Nchumbonga George Lekelefac

Reverend Father Doctorandus Maurice Akwa: 25th Priestly Anniversary Festschrift (15.11.1997 - 15.11.2022), Volume 1. Edited by Nchumbonga George Lekelefac

Reverend Father Doctorandus Maurice Akwa: 25th Priestly Anniversary Festschrift (15.11.1997 - 15.11.2022), Volume 1. Edited by Nchumbonga George Lekelefac

Reverend Father Doctorandus Maurice Akwa: 25th Priestly Anniversary Festschrift (15.11.1997 - 15.11.2022), Volume 1. Edited by Nchumbonga George Lekelefac

Reverend Father Doctorandus Maurice Akwa: 25th Priestly Anniversary Festschrift (15.11.1997 - 15.11.2022), Volume 1. Edited by Nchumbonga George Lekelefac

Reverend Father Doctorandus Maurice Akwa: 25th Priestly Anniversary Festschrift (15.11.1997 - 15.11.2022), Volume 1. Edited by Nchumbonga George Lekelefac

Reverend Father Doctorandus Maurice Akwa: 25th Priestly Anniversary Festschrift (15.11.1997 - 15.11.2022), Volume 1. Edited by Nchumbonga George Lekelefac

Reverend Father Doctorandus Maurice Akwa: 25th Priestly Anniversary Festschrift (15.11.1997 - 15.11.2022), Volume 1. Edited by Nchumbonga George Lekelefac

Reverend Father Doctorandus Maurice Akwa: 25th Priestly Anniversary Festschrift (15.11.1997 - 15.11.2022), Volume 1. Edited by Nchumbonga George Lekelefac

Reverend Father Doctorandus Maurice Akwa: 25th Priestly Anniversary Festschrift (15.11.1997 - 15.11.2022), Volume 1. Edited by Nchumbonga George Lekelefac

Reverend Father Doctorandus Maurice Akwa: 25th Priestly Anniversary Festschrift (15.11.1997 - 15.11.2022), Volume 1. Edited by Nchumbonga George Lekelefac

Reverend Father Doctorandus Maurice Akwa: 25th Priestly Anniversary Festschrift (15.11.1997 - 15.11.2022), Volume 1. Edited by Nchumbonga George Lekelefac

Reverend Father Doctorandus Maurice Akwa: 25th Priestly Anniversary Festschrift (15.11.1997 - 15.11.2022), Volume 1. Edited by Nchumbonga George Lekelefac

Reverend Father Doctorandus Maurice Akwa: 25th Priestly Anniversary Festschrift (15.11.1997 - 15.11.2022), Volume 1. Edited by Nchumbonga George Lekelefac

Reverend Father Doctorandus Maurice Akwa: 25th Priestly Anniversary Festschrift (15.11.1997 - 15.11.2022), Volume 1. Edited by Nchumbonga George Lekelefac

Reverend Father Doctorandus Maurice Akwa: 25th Priestly Anniversary Festschrift (15.11.1997 - 15.11.2022), Volume 1. Edited by Nchumbonga George Lekelefac

Reverend Father Doctorandus Maurice Akwa: 25th Priestly Anniversary Festschrift (15.11.1997 - 15.11.2022), Volume 1. Edited by Nchumbonga George Lekelefac

Reverend Father Doctorandus Maurice Akwa: 25th Priestly Anniversary Festschrift (15.11.1997 - 15.11.2022), Volume 1. Edited by Nchumbonga George Lekelefac

Reverend Father Doctorandus Maurice Akwa: 25th Priestly Anniversary Festschrift (15.11.1997 - 15.11.2022), Volume 1. Edited by Nchumbonga George Lekelefac

Reverend Father Doctorandus Maurice Akwa: 25th Priestly Anniversary Festschrift (15.11.1997 - 15.11.2022), Volume 1. Edited by Nchumbonga George Lekelefac

Reverend Father Doctorandus Maurice Akwa: 25th Priestly Anniversary Festschrift (15.11.1997 - 15.11.2022), Volume 1. Edited by Nchumbonga George Lekelefac

Reverend Father Doctorandus Maurice Akwa: 25th Priestly Anniversary Festschrift (15.11.1997 - 15.11.2022), Volume 1. Edited by Nchumbonga George Lekelefac

Reverend Father Doctorandus Maurice Akwa: 25th Priestly Anniversary Festschrift (15.11.1997 - 15.11.2022), Volume 1. Edited by Nchumbonga George Lekelefac

Reverend Father Doctorandus Maurice Akwa: 25th Priestly Anniversary Festschrift (15.11.1997 - 15.11.2022), Volume 1. Edited by Nchumbonga George Lekelefac

Reverend Father Doctorandus Maurice Akwa: 25th Priestly Anniversary Festschrift (15.11.1997 - 15.11.2022), Volume 1. Edited by Nchumbonga George Lekelefac

Reverend Father Doctorandus Maurice Akwa: 25th Priestly Anniversary Festschrift (15.11.1997 - 15.11.2022), Volume 1. Edited by Nchumbonga George Lekelefac

Reverend Father Doctorandus Maurice Akwa: 25th Priestly Anniversary Festschrift (15.11.1997 - 15.11.2022), Volume 1. Edited by Nchumbonga George Lekelefac

Reverend Father Doctorandus Maurice Akwa: 25th Priestly Anniversary Festschrift (15.11.1997 - 15.11.2022), Volume 1. Edited by Nchumbonga George Lekelefac

Reverend Father Doctorandus Maurice Akwa: 25th Priestly Anniversary Festschrift (15.11.1997 - 15.11.2022), Volume 1. Edited by Nchumbonga George Lekelefac

Reverend Father Doctorandus Maurice Akwa: 25th Priestly Anniversary Festschrift (15.11.1997 - 15.11.2022), Volume 1. Edited by Nchumbonga George Lekelefac

Reverend Father Doctorandus Maurice Akwa: 25th Priestly Anniversary Festschrift (15.11.1997 - 15.11.2022), Volume 1. Edited by Nchumbonga George Lekelefac

Reverend Father Doctorandus Maurice Akwa: 25th Priestly Anniversary Festschrift (15.11.1997 - 15.11.2022), Volume 1. Edited by Nchumbonga George Lekelefac

Reverend Father Doctorandus Maurice Akwa: 25th Priestly Anniversary Festschrift (15.11.1997 - 15.11.2022), Volume 1. Edited by Nchumbonga George Lekelefac

Reverend Father Doctorandus Maurice Akwa: 25th Priestly Anniversary Festschrift (15.11.1997 - 15.11.2022), Volume 1. Edited by Nchumbonga George Lekelefac

Reverend Father Doctorandus Maurice Akwa: 25th Priestly Anniversary Festschrift (15.11.1997 - 15.11.2022), Volume 1. Edited by Nchumbonga George Lekelefac

Reverend Father Doctorandus Maurice Akwa: 25th Priestly Anniversary Festschrift (15.11.1997 - 15.11.2022), Volume 1. Edited by Nchumbonga George Lekelefac

Reverend Father Doctorandus Maurice Akwa: 25th Priestly Anniversary Festschrift (15.11.1997 - 15.11.2022), Volume 1. Edited by Nchumbonga George Lekelefac

END OF VOLUME 1

Made in the USA
Middletown, DE
28 January 2023